AnimalWays

Sharks

AnimalWays

Sharks

BENCHMARK BOOKS

MARSHALL CAVENDISH
NEW YORK

With thanks to Mark F. L. Smith, Curator, Lisbon Aquarium, Portugal,
for his expert reading of this manuscript

Benchmark Books
Marshall Cavendish Corporation
99 White Plains Road
Tarrytown, NY 10591-9001
Website: www.marshallcavendish.com

Library of Congress Cataloging-in-Publication Data
Sieswerda, Paul L.
Sharks / by Paul L. Sieswerda.
p. cm. — (Animal ways)
Includes bibliographical references (p.107) and index.
ISBN 0-7614-1267-0
1.Sharks—Juvenile literature. [1. Sharks.] I. Title. II. Animal ways (Tarrytown, N.Y.)
QL638.9 .S53   2001   597.3—dc21   00-050740

Photo Research by Candlepants, Inc.

Cover photo: Animals Animals/ Henry Ausloos

The photographs in this book are used by permission and through the courtesy of: *Animals
Animals/Earth Scenes*: James Watt, 2-3, 9, 40, 83, 85; Randy Morse, 7, 100; W. Gregory
Brown, 13; E.R. Degginger, 21; Bruce Watkins, 24 (top left), 28 (top); George Bernard, 24
(top right), 36; Bob Cranston, 29 (lower), 38, 43, 51; Tim Rock, 45; Carl Roessler, 55, 95; P.
Kay, 62; H. Hall, 67. *Jeff Rotman Photography*: Jeff Rotman, 11, 12 (upper), 17, 31, 35, 37,
47, 52, 57, 58, 59, 61, 63, 69, 76, 78, 81, 91, 93; Doug Perrine, back cover; Koji Nakamura,
12 (lower); Bruce Rasner, 70; © *Jonathon Bird*/ORG: 15, 28 (center), 29 (top & center), 33,
65, 88; *Innerspace Visions*: Richard Hermann, 22; Doug Perrine, 24 (lower); Marty
Snyderman, 28 (lower); Norburt Wu, 73; Gwen Lowe, 73 (inset); David Wrobel, 74.

Printed in Italy

1 3 5 6 4 2

Contents

1 The World of Sharks   8
Shark Habitats

2 Is a Shark a Fish—or Not?   16
The Unchanging Shark • Bony Fishes • The Earliest Sharks •
The Relatives • The Living Sharks

3 Shark Design   32
Shark Skeletons • Shark Teeth • Keeping Afloat •
Tails and Fins • Shark Muscles • Gills and Breathing •
Diverse Species, Similar Body Forms

4 Shark Senses   46
Sound • Smell • Electroreception • Taste

5 Shark Ways   54
Shark Studies • What We've Learned •
Mating and Reproduction

6 A Gallery of Sharks   66
The Big • The Strange • The Deadly

7 Sharks and Us   82
International Shark Attack File • Sharks As Food •
Protecting Sharks • Living with Sharks •
Statistics—Help or Hindrance? • Save the Sharks

GLOSSARY 102 · SPECIES CHECKLIST 104 · FURTHER RESEARCH 106 ·
BIBLIOGRAPHY 108 · INDEX 109

HERE ARE SOME OF THE MAIN PHYLA, CLASSES, AND ORDERS, WITH PHOTOGRAPHS OF
A TYPICAL ANIMAL FROM EACH GROUP.

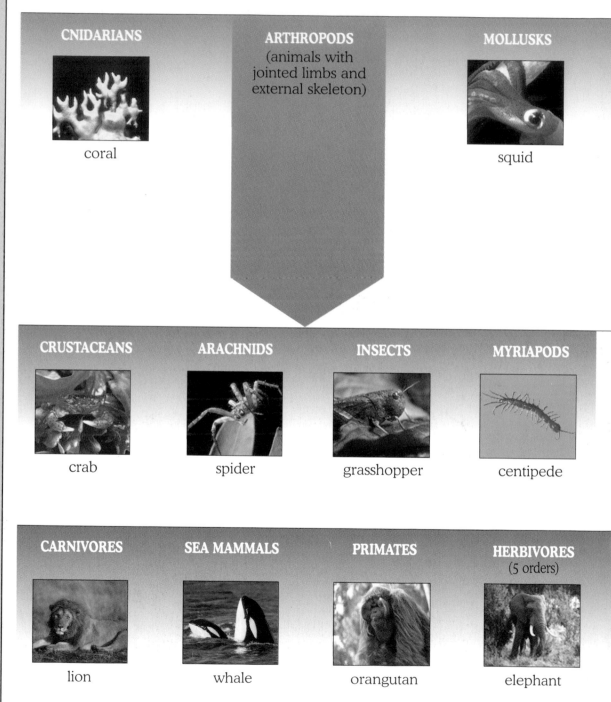

Animal Kingdom

CNIDARIANS

coral

ARTHROPODS
(animals with
jointed limbs and
external skeleton)

MOLLUSKS

squid

CRUSTACEANS

crab

ARACHNIDS

spider

INSECTS

grasshopper

MYRIAPODS

centipede

CARNIVORES

lion

SEA MAMMALS

whale

PRIMATES

orangutan

HERBIVORES
(5 orders)

elephant

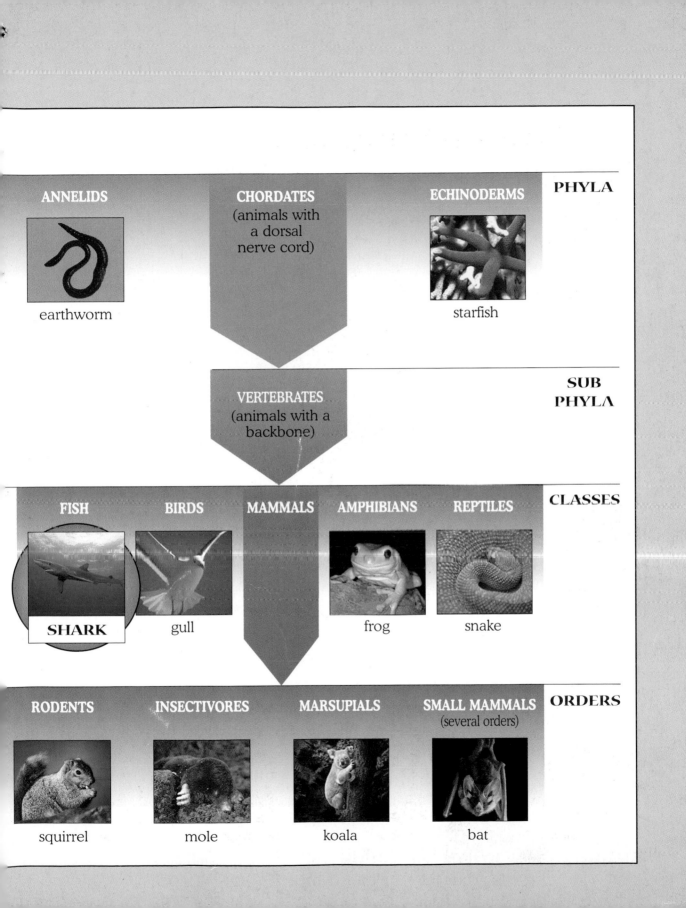

PHYLA

ANNELIDS

earthworm

CHORDATES
(animals with
a dorsal
nerve cord)

ECHINODERMS

starfish

SUB PHYLA

VERTEBRATES
(animals with a
backbone)

CLASSES

FISH

SHARK

BIRDS

gull

MAMMALS

AMPHIBIANS

frog

REPTILES

snake

ORDERS

RODENTS

squirrel

INSECTIVORES

mole

MARSUPIALS

koala

SMALL MAMMALS
(several orders)

bat

1 The World of Sharks

> "HE WAS A VERY BIG MAKO SHARK BUILT TO SWIM AS FAST AS THE FASTEST FISH IN THE SEA AND EVERYTHING ABOUT HIM WAS BEAUTIFUL EXCEPT HIS JAWS."
>
> From *The Old Man and the Sea*,
> Ernest Hemingway

It's summer at the seashore. The bright afternoon sun sparkles on the waves that crash hard on the packed sand. Children run ahead of the thin layer of sea foam that slides up the beach. Beyond the surf line, in calmer waters where your feet still touch the bottom, you feel safe. Yet you think, "What else could be in the water? . . . A shark?" That shuddering thought has passed through virtually every swimmer's mind since the movie *Jaws* was released. Probably swimmers had felt the same even centuries before. The movie's success is due, in some part, to that universal fear.

ONE OF THE MOST VORACIOUS SHARKS, THE TIGER SHARK PREYS ON FISH, SEA TURTLES, OTHER SHARKS, AND SOMETIMES HUMANS.

But is that fear realistic or imaginary? Sharks, of course, do share the same ocean waters with swimmers and sometimes they have been known to attack humans. The flash of fear that people experience is due to the fact that most of them know sharks can be dangerous. And it's only a flash because most people also know that the chance of shark attack is rare. Death by shark attack is rarer than by a lightning strike or a bee sting, and certainly far rarer than by an automobile accident. In fact, it is estimated that only about one hundred people each year are attacked by sharks worldwide. And only about fifteen of those attacks are fatal. Of course, if you or someone you know is one of those victims, "only" seems like the wrong word. Sharks can be dangerous, just like lightning, bees, and automobiles. However, just as knowing about automobiles and safety reduces the risk and helps people use them wisely, understanding which types of sharks are dangerous, when a threat is real, and how to be cautious can reduce fear and replace it with respect.

Shark Habitats

Oceans cover most of the earth's surface. The average depth in the sea is more than two miles (3 km). Sharks live throughout this vast expanse, from warm tropical waters where humans commonly share the wet space to the frigid waters beneath the Arctic ice. In fact, estimates indicate that sharks are the most abundant of all large animals in the ocean.

The most familiar species of sharks are found along coastlines in fairly shallow, or littoral, depths. Some live on the bottom. Those that inhabit such areas are usually sluggish and sedentary. Others live in the open, or pelagic, seas and are designed for fast swimming. The oceans are so vast and cover so many different zones of temperature, depth, and light that it is difficult to describe

Scientists around the world study sharks. This scientist is examining a juvenile hammerhead in Hawaii. Baby sharks are called "pups."

A COUNTER-IMAGE

Sharks come in all shapes and sizes and not all of them are dangerous. In fact, some are almost laughable as a threat to humans. The smallest known shark—the pygmy shark—is eleven inches (27 cm) long; the two largest—the whale shark at forty feet (13.3 m) and the basking shark at thirty (10 m)—are almost toothless giants that feed on small fishes and plankton. Some sharks stay on the bottom and crunch shrimp and lobsters. Others chase down some of the fastest fish in the sea.

BASKING SHARKS STRAIN HUGE AMOUNTS OF WATER THROUGH THEIR ENORMOUS MOUTHS. AMONG THE LARGEST SHARKS, THEY FEED ON THE SMALLEST FOODS.

CAT SHARKS ARE AMONG THE SMALLEST SPECIES. THEY LIVE MOSTLY ON THE BOTTOM AND FEED ON SMALL FISH AND CRUSTACEANS.

SHARKS LIKE THIS CARIBBEAN REEF SHARK ARE ADAPTED TO SWIM OVER REEFS IN TROPICAL WATERS.

a typical shark and where it lives. Sharks are a very successful group of animals that have adapted to habitats throughout the marine seas and even some freshwater lakes and rivers—such as the lakes and rivers in Nicaragua, which are home to bull sharks.

Sharks have lived without much change in their basic form

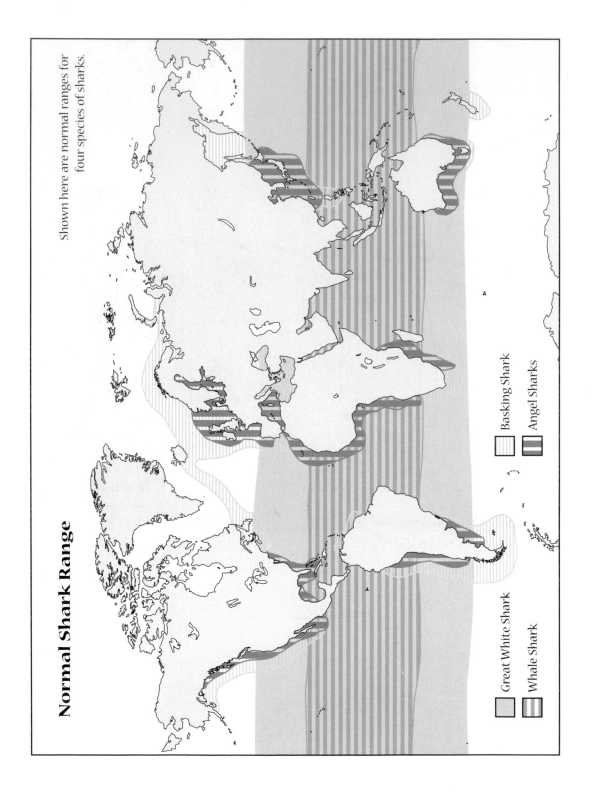

Normal Shark Range

Shown here are normal ranges for four species of sharks.

Great White Shark

Whale Shark

Basking Shark

Angel Sharks

for millions of years. This is due to the fact that their habitat had remained fairly constant. The ocean is so big that changes occur extremely slowly. Today, though, this environment is being threatened and is changing rapidly—and sharks do not have the millions of years needed to adapt to these new conditions.

NURSE SHARKS ARE SLUGGISH. THEY LOOK LIKE GIANT TADPOLES AND SOMETIMES REST STACKED ONE ON TOP OF THE OTHER.

2 Is a Shark a Fish—or Not?

A shark is a fish but a fish is not necessarily a shark. It is said that sharks have remained the same for millions of years. While the basic form of sharks has been very successful and has remained largely unchanged, different species have come and gone throughout their evolutionary history. Modern-day sharks are simply the result of the evolutionary process that enables them to fill their specific niche. Their origins are actually more recent than bony fishes'. Fish are animals that have backbones and gills. As such, all sharks are fish. However, some fishes have backbones made of bone and others have skeletons made of

THE PROTRUDING JAW OF THE GREAT WHITE SHARK, STUDDED WITH SCALPEL-SHARP TEETH, IS ONE OF THE ADAPTATIONS THAT MAKES THIS SHARK A SUCCESSFUL PREDATOR.

cartilage. Cartilage is the material that makes up your ears and nose. It is firm, but not as hard as bone. Cartilaginous fishes are the sharks, rays, and their remote cousins the chimaeras.

The Unchanging Shark

Sharks have been on earth for about 400 million years. In comparison, human history is a brief moment of less than two million years. During the sharks' time span, the dinosaurs and trilobites—the ancestors of insects, crabs, and spiders that dominated the seas—disappeared from the land. In some cases, sharks are little changed from forms that swam in prehistoric seas.

In fact, sharks that lived during the early Devonian period (410 to 360 million years ago) had the same shape as many of today's species. The fossil remains of a prehistoric shark called *Cladoselache* was found preserved in rocks that are 375 million years old. The shark was about three feet (1 m) long. It had slender jaws with pointed teeth and a tail shaped much like that of fast-swimming sharks of today.

Bony Fishes

Scientists once thought that bony fish had evolved from an earlier form of fish having a cartilage skeleton. Later this was proved to be incorrect. The first bony fishes came in the many forms of jawless and armor-plated species.

Before the appearance of sharks, in the early Paleozoic period (500 million years ago), jawless fishes, or ostracoderms, were widespread. They had bony skeletons and hence were among the earliest vertebrates. Some, such as the hagfish and lampreys, still exist and are able to eat without having jaws.

Shark Relationships

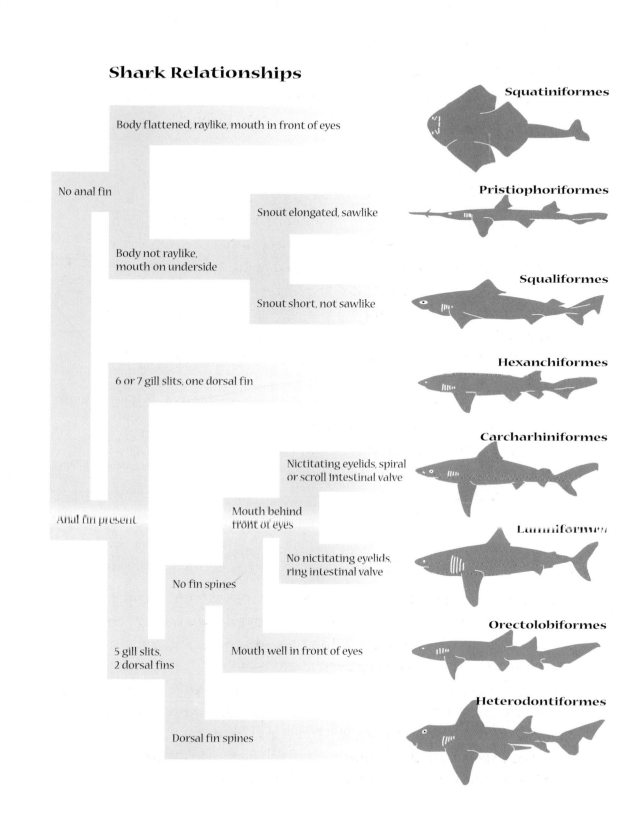

Squatiniformes

Body flattened, raylike, mouth in front of eyes

No anal fin

Pristiophoriformes

Snout elongated, sawlike

Body not raylike,
mouth on underside

Snout short, not sawlike

Squaliformes

6 or 7 gill slits, one dorsal fin

Hexanchiformes

Carcharhiniformes

Nictitating eyelids, spiral
or scroll intestinal valve

Mouth behind
front of eyes

Anal fin present

Lamniformes

No nictitating eyelids,
ring intestinal valve

No fin spines

Orectolobiformes

5 gill slits,
2 dorsal fins

Mouth well in front of eyes

Heterodontiformes

Dorsal fin spines

The early fishes did have openings for a mouth, but their mouths could not move to bite or chew as jaws do. Jaws that grip prey, defend against predators, and manipulate food particles in the mouth are a great advantage that developed in fishes over time.

Some of these fishes grew to huge sizes. Often, in those early seas, sharks were prey, rather than predators.

The Earliest Sharks

The age of some fossil teeth shows that sharks existed long before *Cladoselache*. No imprint of an earlier shark's body has been found yet. However, microscopic fossil scales, which are all that remain of the earliest sharks, indicate an even earlier history.

The bodies of sharks are covered with miniature toothlike structures, called denticles. Like human teeth, they are hard enough to be preserved in the fossil record. The evidence of these denticles dates back 450 million years.

The shark's flexible skeleton of cartilage seems to be a modification of the heavy, brittle skeletons of bony fishes. This modification has worked well up to the present day. By the time of the dinosaurs, sharks were a dominant life-form in the seas.

The Relatives

Scientists classify all life-forms into groups that are based on common characteristics and evolutionary history. Sharks have backbones. As such they are grouped into the phylum Chordata, which includes all the vertebrate animals—fishes, amphibians, reptiles, birds, and mammals. Of the fishes, there are two major classes: the Osteichthyes (fish that have a bony skeleton) and the Chondrichthyes (fish that have a skeleton made of cartilage).

WHAT FOSSILS REVEAL

SHARK TEETH, SUCH AS THIS MASSIVE EXAMPLE FROM THE EXTINCT *CARCHARODON MEGALODON*, ARE THE SHARK'S ONLY BODY PARTS HARD ENOUGH TO BE FOUND IN THE FOSSIL RECORD.

Fossils are mineralized skeletons or impressions, such as footprints, made by prehistoric animals while they were alive or of their bodies after they died. Just as you may have printed your initials in the wet cement of a new sidewalk, prehistoric animals sometimes left a similar imprint. When ancient sea animals died they would fall into the mud. The hard, or bony, parts of their bodies left an impression. The mud eventually became rock, and the image of the life-form was preserved. The only records of sharks that lived before *Cladoselache* are teeth. Shark teeth are very common for fossil hunters to find. There are many places where one can go and expect to find at least a handful of fossil shark teeth in a day's time. Fossils give scientists a picture of the earth's history. Scientists can date the age of the rock and so learn when that animal lived. This is called the fossil record. Sometimes the fossil record even shows how the animal lived. For example, some fossils of Cladoselache have fossils of other, smaller fish inside them. The fossils show that Cladoselache had swallowed the smaller fish, tail first—confirming the fact that these sharks were fast enough to chase down their prey.

This cartilage skeleton is found in sharks and in some other groups of closely related species.

Chimaeras. The chimaeras, which date back about 300 million years, are examples of a line of fish that are closely related to sharks. The only chimaeras existing today are the rattails. These are strange, deep-dwelling fish with pointed snouts and teeth like rats. They have a large spine in front of the dorsal fin and a hook

THE CHIMAERA, OR RATTAIL, IS A SPECIES THAT REMAINS FROM A ONCE ABUNDANT FAMILY OF SHARKS. ITS STRANGE SHAPE SEEMS LIKE A MIXTURE OF SEVERAL ANIMALS.

on the forehead that is used in mating. It is little wonder that this fish is named after the mythical Chimera, a fire-breathing monster the Greeks envisioned as having the head of a lion, the body of a goat, and the tail of a dragon. Fortunately, the fish that lives today is not commonly more than two to three feet (60 to 90 cm) long.

Skates, rays, and sawfish. Another group closely related to the sharks is Batoidei. This group includes skates, rays, and sawfish, recent forms that have evolved from the shark line since the Jurassic period (208 to 144 million years ago). There are about 470 species, which makes this group more numerous than the sharks themselves. Their size varies from as small as four inches (10 cm) to the giant manta ray, which has a wingspan of more than eighteen feet (6 m). Essentially, they are all flattened sharks. Their pectoral fins are flattened and enlarged. In some species, such as in many of the rays, the pectoral fins act as wings, allowing the fish to "fly" through the water. The manta ray, with a wingspan of up to fourteen feet (4.3 m), strains plankton through its gaping mouth as it moves through the surface waters of tropical seas. In other species, the pectoral fins are flattened to accommodate a life on the bottom.

The Batoidei take in water through holes on the top of their head so they can pass water over their gills to breathe. These holes are called spiracles. This enables them to lie unmoving in the sand, completely hidden. Most other sharks, who breathe through gills located behind their heads, must swim in order to keep water passing over the gills.

Members of the Batoidei group seldom use the tail for propulsion. As a result, the tail often has been reduced to a whiplike appendage. Some rays have a venomous spine along the tail that is good protection against predators and can be a serious danger to humans.

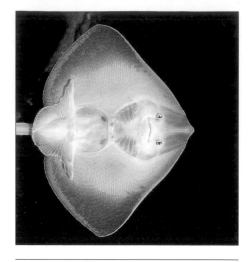

THIS MANTA RAY IS A RELATIVE OF THE SHARK. ITS PEC-TORAL FINS HAVE BECOME HUGE WINGS AND ITS TAIL IS REDUCED TO A WHIPLIKE APPENDAGE. SOME RAYS HAVE A VENOMOUS SPINE IN THEIR TAILS.

SKATES ARE FLATTENED FOR LIFE ON THE BOTTOM. THE MOUTH IS ON THE UNDER-SIDE (SHOWN HERE) WHILE THE EYES ARE ON THE TOP, ALONG WITH SMALL OPEN-INGS, CALLED SPIRACLES, THAT TAKE IN WATER. WATER PASSES OVER THE GILLS (THE RED STRUCTURE) AND OUT THE UNDERSIDE GILL SLITS.

THE SAWFISH'S SNOUT IS STUDDED WITH SHARP TEETH. THE TEETH CAN FLAY A SCHOOL OF FISH INTO BITE-SIZED PIECES. THE SAWFISH IS SHAPED MUCH LIKE A SHARK BUT FLATTENED LIKE A RAY. IT IS CLASSED WITH RAYS AND SKATES.

This diverse group uses varied means for defense and hunting. Sawfish have a tooth-studded snout that can chop a school of fish into pieces. Some rays have electric organs that produce powerful shocks to discourage predators or stun prey; others rely on camouflage to hide from predators or to stalk prey.

The Living Sharks

The approximately 350 species of living sharks are generally grouped into eight basic forms, or orders, according to special features. For instance, the location of fins and mouth and the presence of spines are all clues to how closely one shark is related to another. Members of the eight orders are then separated according to external features and placed in even more descriptive groups called families. For instance, some species of sharks have an anal fin and others do not. Some that have an anal fin have more than five gill slits, so they are further separated from sharks that have more or fewer gill slits. There are thirty families of sharks known today.

By listing and then grouping sharks according to these kinds of characteristics, scientists can identify the various species and often learn their evolutionary history. We will examine the eight orders of sharks.

Angel sharks. One shark order is the Squatiniformes—the angel sharks. All the angel sharks are in one family. As is true of most sharks, the angel shark's shape tells a great deal about its natural history, or how it lives its life. Angel sharks have a flattened shape, which indicates that these sharks spend much of their life on or near the bottom of the ocean. Their tail fins are soft, with weak muscles. Angel sharks are not fast swimmers and rely on camouflage to help them catch prey or hide from predators. Except for the important fact that their pectoral fins are not attached to their heads, these sharks look like their cousins, the skates and rays.

Saw sharks. The saw sharks are a small order of sharks called Pristiophoriformes. They resemble the more modern sawfishes. Sawsharks have a flat bladelike snout that is edged with sharp teeth. They have two long barbels, or feelers. These sensors assist them in their bottom living. They differ from sawfish in that their gills are on the sides of their bodies rather than underneath.

Six- or Seven-gill sharks. Another order of living sharks is the six- or seven-gill sharks, or Hexanchiformes. Unlike all other sharks, which have five gill openings, the Hexanchiformes have six or seven. One species, called the frilled shark, looks very primitive, with an eel-like body and frilly edges on the gill openings.

Many species in this group are deep-water sharks that prefer cold temperatures. Some can grow to a large size. For example, the bluntnose six-gill can reach fifteen feet (4.5 m).

Mackerel sharks. The Lamniformes, or mackerel sharks, are fast swimmers. Their bodies are shaped like the fuselage of a jet plane. Their tail fin is crescent-shaped, hard, and attached to strong muscles. The mako shark even has a keel, much like another speed demon, the swordfish. This is a ridge that sticks out horizontally just in front of the tail. The mako's keel helps it control its motion at great speeds. Designers of nuclear attack submarines have used models of fast-swimming sharks to construct vessels that can move as swiftly underwater as many surface ships can above the waves.

Carpet sharks and Horned sharks. Sharks with mouths that do not extend behind their eyes are either in the order Orectolobiformes or Heterodontiformes.

Heterodontiformes, or horned sharks, have spines in front of their dorsal fins. This small group contains the Port Jackson shark and the horned shark of California.

The Orectolobiformes, or carpet sharks, have mouths that are good for sucking prey out of crevices. Their teeth are usually small and most of them are harmless. However, they can bite. The wobbegong of Australia, for example, is known for its bulldoglike bite. Another carpet shark is the giant whale shark. As an open-water swimmer, it is not typical of carpet sharks. However, since its large mouth is in front of the eyes and it has no spines in front of its dorsal fin, it is placed in this group.

Ground sharks. The largest order of sharks, and the one most people envision as "typical," is Carcharhiniformes, or ground sharks. These sharks probably earned their name because of where they are usually caught or seen: near the bottom, on fishing grounds. This group contains most of the ocean-dwelling sharks, such as the blue shark and the oceanic whitetips.

Most of the sharks that are dangerous to humans belong to this group. One family, the Carcharhinidae, is known by another name, the requiem sharks. A requiem is a memorial service or hymn for the souls of the dead. This is an appropriate name for these sharks because they have caused the deaths of many people. Within this family, tiger, bull, lemon, and many reef sharks have been involved in attacks. These sharks are often found in coastal waters, where humans are likely to be swimming, fishing, or scuba diving. Other dangerous sharks, such as the oceanic whitetip, are not often in contact with people because they live in the middle of the ocean. However, they have been known to attack the survivors of shipwrecks or of troopships torpedoed during wartime.

The strange-looking hammerhead shark is in this group. So are many harmless sharks, such as the cat sharks, which live off the east coast of the United States, and the leopard shark, which is found off the coast of California.

The ground sharks differ from the mackerel sharks in that

Sharks are so varied that no typical form represents them all. From the giant whale shark cruising the open seas with attendant pilot fish to the illusive angel shark blending into rocks on the ocean floor, each species has found a successful way to live. Here are examples of species belonging to six orders. The order is given in Latin, followed by the common species name.

Squatiniforme: angel shark

Orectolobiforme:
whale shark

Pristiophoriforme: saw shark

Heterodontiforme:
horned shark

Lamniforme: mako shark

Carcharhiniforme: Galapagos shark

WHAT'S IN A NAME?

The process of putting a specimen into an order for scientific classification is called taxonomy, or scientific nomenclature (naming). While scientists argue about what specimens go where, and sometimes change their names because of new information, this system does help identify all plants and animals. It gives some organization to the relationships between species, their evolution, and even their behavior. As DNA testing grows as a technique of identification, these relationships will become clearer and more precise. The scientific names may seem difficult, but usually they are meaningful and descriptive.

Almost everyone knows the name Tyrannosaurus rex. These names come from Latin and Greek roots: Tyrannos - tyrant, sauros - lizard, rex - king. "King of the tyrant lizards" is a meaningful name for this mighty dinosaur. The same is true for the spiny dogfish, Squalus acanthias. It is a shark with spines in front of each dorsal fin, and its scientific name indicates this: Squalus = sea fish, acanth = thorn.

The most important feature of scientific nomenclature is that it provides a name for a particular species that everyone will recognize. For example, "sand shark" is a common name that can mean different fish to different people depending on where they live. In the northeastern United States, people call the spiny dogfish "sand shark." But farther south, in New Jersey, a sand shark is considered a different fish altogether. However, every scientist throughout the world, no matter his or her native language, calls this species Squalus acanthias

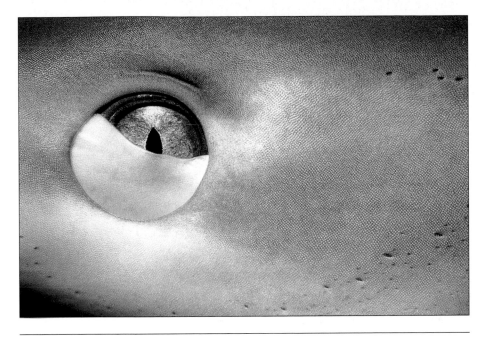

THIS GROUND SHARK IS FEEDING. ITS NICTITATING MEMBRANE IS HALF-CLOSED TO PROTECT THE EYE.

they have a special nictitating eyelid. This is a transparent membrane that acts as an extra eyelid. When ground sharks bite, the nictitating eyelids protect their eyes during any struggle with prey.

Dogfish sharks. A scientist or even a knowledgeable student might catch a common spiny dogfish and wonder to what order this shark belongs. By knowing the classification by order, he or she can figure this out. The spiny dogfish does not have an anal fin, so it does not belong in any of the orders that do. That narrows it down. But maybe it could be in the order Squatiniformes. No, because its body is not flattened. Nor does it have a sawlike snout like Pristiophoriformes. Therefore, it must be in the order Squaliformes, the dogfish sharks.

3 Shark Design

> As Little Red Riding Hood went near the bed, she said, "My, what big eyes you have, Grandma." The wolf said, "All the better to see you with, my dear."
>
> *Little Red Riding Hood*, The Brothers Grimm

Sharks have often been described as perfectly designed eating machines. Because their teeth are so prominent, and in some cases so awesome, it is natural to focus on the shark's eating ability. However, any animal that survives must be a perfectly designed eating machine as well as a perfectly designed reproduction machine, escape artist, hunter, and, in general, survivor. This is as true for sharks, lions, eagles, and other great predators as it is for the prey species that graze on the vegetation of the open grasslands or the ocean's plankton. The species that exist

Sharks like this sand tiger have evolved into a form well suited for survival. This shark, common along the Atlantic coast, is harmless to humans.

today have bodies and behaviors designed for a world in which eat-or-be-eaten is the law.

Sharks have had to adapt in order to survive. Some hunting methods may be as dramatic and forceful as those of the great white, or as quiet and slow as the behavior of the basking shark, which simply strains shrimp and other small creatures called plankton through its mouth as it swims through the surface waters.

Shark Skeletons

The shark's body is supported by a skeleton made of cartilage. Cartilage is lighter and more flexible than bone. Humans have cartilage in their noses and ears, and also between bony joints like the knees, where it is used as a shock absorber. It is thought that the shark's skeleton evolved from the bony skeletons of fishes that existed around 450 million years ago. Those fishes were heavy and clad in thick bone acting as protective armor, which became a disadvantage. Just as medieval knights were often overcome by quick-moving soldiers, these bony-plated fishes were replaced by quicker sharks and bony fish that had evolved lighter, more flexible skeletons and better maneuverability.

Cartilage decays after an animal dies. You can see that by looking at a human skull. There is a hole where the nose was once located; the bony skull remains but the nose decomposes. Because sharks do not have bony skeletons, very few remains of prehistoric sharks have been found. However, sometimes sharks died and fell into special areas where their bodies were covered with silt, or fine sand. The silt kept the body from decomposing, and over time the shark's complete form was preserved as a fossil. It is the record of these rare fossils that gives scientists a view of the early history of sharks.

Shark Teeth. Shark's teeth are highly evolved forms of similar hard structures found on a shark's skin. Called dermal denticles, they cover a shark's body in the same way scales cover most bony fishes. These "skin teeth" are tiny but rough. Victims of shark attacks are often scraped when the shark's skin brushes their body. Before sandpaper, carpenters and cabinetmakers used sharkskin, or shagreen, to achieve a smooth finish.

During the shark's evolution, the rows of dermal denticles became teeth of various shapes and sizes. Some are flattened plates that crush the shells of mollusks. Others are sharp and pointed for gripping slippery fish. The cookie-cutter shark, for instance, has a ring of sharp teeth that cuts perfect little circles

THE SAND TIGER SHARK HAS A FEARSOME MOUTH, YET ITS SLENDER, POINTED TEETH ARE DESIGNED TO GRASP ONLY SLIPPERY FISH.

out of the skin of whales. But the most terrifying teeth are those of the large predators, such as great whites, tigers, hammerheads, and bull sharks. These are sharp cutting blades. Sometimes they are serrated like steak knives. They are used for slicing into large prey such as whales, sea lions, sea turtles, or, in rare instances, human beings. In any case, such teeth cut horribly into the prey.

When a shark loses any of its teeth, in struggles with its prey or with age, rows of new teeth grow in to replace the lost ones. It has been estimated that a shark may lose and replace more than ten thousand teeth during its lifetime.

Because sharks' teeth, unlike their cartilaginous skeletons, are hard and lasting, they are preserved in great numbers in many places around the world. Sometimes these areas are far

THE TEETH OF THE MAKO SHARK ARE SIMILAR TO THE SAND TIGER'S, BUT THEY ARE STRONGER AND ABLE TO BITE LARGE FISH, SUCH AS TUNA OR SWORDFISH.

A MIGHTY PREHISTORIC PREDATOR

The most fearsome predator the earth has known is not a killer whale, a lion, a tiger, or a great white shark. It is not even those well-known prehistoric dinosaurs, Tyrannosaurus rex, or Velociraptor. It is a shark called Carcharodon megalodon. An extinct relative of the great white, this incredible creature was about fifty feet (15 m) long and weighed perhaps fifty tons. This is comparable to that of the great whales, but Carcharodon megalodon had jaws filled with serrated teeth eight inches (20 cm) long! There is some evidence that this shark lived as recently as fifty thousand years ago.

Some new animals have been discovered in modern times. For example, the coelacanth is a fish that was thought to be extinct for 70 million years. It was found living in the waters of South Africa in 1938. The existence of a large shark called the megamouth was not discovered until 1976.

The ocean is such a vast space that no one

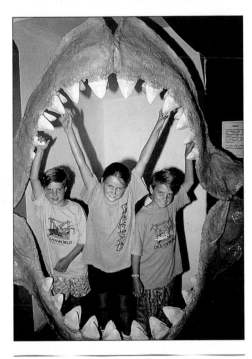

THE MOUTH OF THE PREHISTORIC SHARK, *CARCHARODON MEGALONDON*, IS TERRIBLE TO IMAGINE. MEGALONDON MEANS "GIANT TOOTH."

can be sure what does or does not live in its depths. Some people wonder if a shark like Carcharodon megalodon could still be alive. It is an exciting and fearful thought, but there is no evidence that it does, and the only clues that remain are its fossil teeth. The teeth are fairly common in the fossil record. They show up in many parts of the world, which indicates that this must have been an abundant species at one time. Carcharodon megalodon fed on large prey, perhaps early whales. We still have whales, but there is no record of any modern whales having been attacked by an animal bigger than a killer whale or great white shark.

The modern great white shark has serrated teeth that are similar in shape to those of the Carcharodon megalodon. It is likely they were close relatives. It is reasonable to picture Carcharodon megalodon as a giant great white shark, both in shape and in behavior—a super predator.

away from today's oceans. Throughout time the continents have risen and fallen so that what are mountain ranges today were once the bottom of ancient seas. One such place is in North America, where a shallow inland sea covered much of what is now the north and middle of the United States. The area is now a rich collecting area for fossil teeth and occasionally a complete ancient shark specimen.

ROWS OF NEW TEETH ARE READY TO REPLACE THOSE LOST IN THE STRUGGLES OF THE HUNT. THE SERRATED EDGES OF THIS TIGER SHARK'S TEETH ARE GOOD FOR CUTTING THROUGH LARGE OBJECTS.

Keeping Afloat

Modern bony fishes developed an organ called a swim bladder. This contains gas that adds buoyancy and offsets their heavy skeletons. Sharks do not have a swim bladder. Rather, they have a large oily liver that serves a similar purpose. In addition to its digestive function, the shark's liver gives it buoyancy, because the oils and fats stored in it are lighter than water. Some livers, like that of the blue shark, can make up as much as twenty percent of a shark's body weight. These sharks swim in the surface waters over deep oceans, so, it is important for them to stay afloat. Basking sharks also have large livers and were once hunted for the organs, which yielded as much as four hundred gallons (1,500 l) of oil.

Tails and Fins

A shark's tail does more than just push the shark through the water. Together with its fins, the tail provides lift and steering while the shark swims. It is often thought that a shark will sink and die if it doesn't keep moving. For many species this is true. It is also true that very few sharks can back up. Certainly none actually swim backward and it is only those bottom dwellers like the nurse or cat sharks that are able to wiggle backward. Some of the faster-swimming sharks, such as the mako and other mackerel sharks, rely on power to attain lift. They are the jet fighters of the shark world, pushing through the water at speeds that are estimated to be as great as forty-three miles (69 km/hr) per hour. Sharks need the lift supplied by the pectoral fins or else they sink. Some sharks must constantly swim forward. However, like birds, they can save some energy by gliding. A "swim-glide" pattern has been observed in aquariums—a slight flick of the tail sends the shark higher. Then the shark slowly glides lower, until it needs to flick its tail again.

Each species finds a system that works. The angel shark is a bottom dweller. It has less need for buoyancy and more body weight than the free swimmers. One shark, the sand tiger, keeps

THE WIDE SPAN OF THE OCEANIC WHITE TIP SHARK DEMONSTRATES HOW SHARKS USE THEIR PECTORAL FINS AS "WINGS" TO GLIDE THROUGH THE WATER. THIS SHARK IS NAMED *CARCHARHINUS LONGIMANUS*, OR "LONG HANDS."

a gulp of air in its stomach to help it cruise at a slow speed without sinking.

Shark Muscles

Sharks have two types of muscle tissue: red muscle and white muscle. Red muscle is filled with a food supply of oxygen-rich blood. This gives sharks the energy to sustain an effort over a long length of time. White muscle has a poor blood supply and functions well only in quick bursts of speed. Sharks with more white muscle than red are poor game fish since after a brief struggle they become exhausted and are mere "deadweight" for the fisherman to pull aboard.

Mackerel sharks, on the other hand, are great game fish. The mako is capable of high leaps out of the water that rival those of a marlin or sailfish. Also like those bony fish, the mackerel sharks have evolved an elevated body temperature that helps their muscles operate more efficiently. This is a remarkable, and only recently discovered, ability in cold-blooded animals. Fish, amphibians, and reptiles usually have the body temperature of the environment around them. That is why they are

Shark muscles

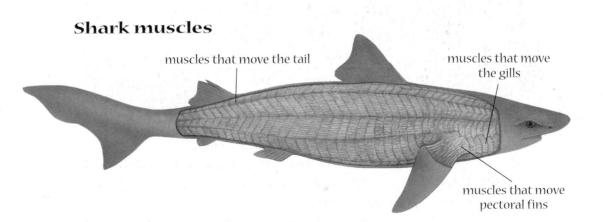

muscles that move the tail

muscles that move the gills

muscles that move pectoral fins

Shark organs

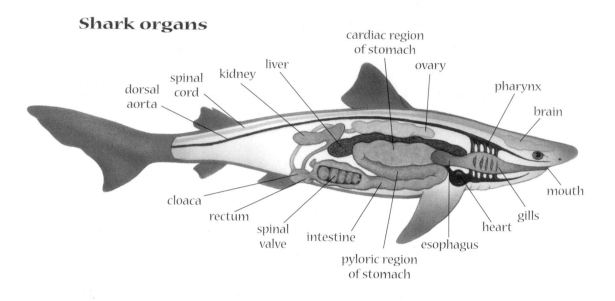

called cold-blooded. Mackerels, however, have a capillary network, called a counter-current exchange system, that acts as a heat exchanger to reduce heat loss and thereby raise the body temperature 9 to 15 degrees Fahrenheit (5–8°C) above the temperature of the surrounding water. The mackerel shark's capillaries, which are tiny blood vessels, spread into a thin layer that warms the blood as it travels from the exterior of the body to the active muscles.

Gills and Breathing. Oxygen is the crucial gas that enables the body's cells to work. Like all fish, sharks must respire, or breathe, underwater. They must obtain oxygen from the water and distribute it throughout the body. The oxygen dissolved in the ocean is produced primarily by the phytoplankton. These "ocean grasses" generate oxygen through photosynthesis in the same manner that grasses, plants, and trees do on land.

To make use of the oxygen and eliminate carbon dioxide and other waste products, sharks pass water over their gills. Sharks take water in through the mouth and pass it out through the slits along the sides of the head. The gills are made up of cartilaginous arches that support gill filaments. These structures are filled with blood vessels. Within the gill filaments are flat platelike structures called secondary lamellae. Blood flows through the secondary lamellae in a direction opposite to the flow of water. This makes the taking in of oxygen and the dumping out of carbon dioxide more efficient.

Many sharks must swim forward with their mouths open to force water over their gills. This is called ramjet ventilation and is common in fast-swimming species. These species must swim continually in order to breathe, which accounts for the once popular belief that all sharks would die if they stopped swimming. However, bottom dwellers, such as nurse sharks, have muscular gill openings that pump water through the gill slits.

GREAT QUANTITIES OF WATER CAN BE PASSED THROUGH THE GILLS OF THIS WHALE SHARK.

These are openings that allow the exit of water that has passed over the gills. Bony fishes and some sharks have a single gill opening covered by a plate called an operculum. This plate actively pumps water through the gills. Even some of the cruising sharks of the reef have been found at rest in caves, pumping water over their gills. Most sharks have five gill slits; a few have six or even seven slits. Shark jaws seem to have evolved as a modification of the first gill arches of early sharks. The frilled shark, an eel-like creature of deep water, may illustrate an evolutionary transition. Its upper jaw is strongly attached to its cranium, or skull, and its mouth is at the front of the head rather than underneath it as in most modern species. Jaws in modern sharks are loosely attached and can protrude outward. It was once thought that sharks had to roll onto their backs in order to bite. This is not true.

Diverse Species, Similar Body Forms

Shark tails often look like those of bony fish. When the body also looks the same, one can safely assume that the two types of fishes probably have similar lifestyles. The mackerel sharks and the fast-swimming game fish (such as marlin, sailfish, and tuna) are quite similar. These animals chase down swift prey—in some cases, each other.

The slow, but strong-swimming, basking sharks have gill rakers that strain plankton for food. These are similar to the baleen plates of the great whales, which also feed on plankton. The whale shark is like a whale in size and behavior, except that its tail is vertical rather than horizontal.

This process of very diverse species developing similar body forms is called convergent evolution. While the crescent shape of some sharks' tails may look like the tuna's, the shark's tail is very different in its evolution and construction. The vertebrae of bony fishes stop at the base of the tail while in sharks it continues into the tail's upper lobe.

The firm support of the backbone gives strength to the flexible cartilage in the shark's back-and-forth swimming thrusts. Different species sometimes have quite distinctive tails. The tail of the thresher shark is exceptional: The upper lobe is almost as long as its whole body. Threshers are believed to use their long tails to herd and perhaps stun schools of fish in a whiplike fashion.

As in the case of the thresher shark, the shape of its tail can often tell about the animal's behavior. A tail with a strong upper lobe and a weak flap on the lower is likely a weak swimmer, such as the nurse shark. This kind of tail is called heterocercal. Homocercal is the term used when each lobe is equal, as is the tail of the porbeagle, a fish-catching shark of cooler waters.

THE NURSE SHARK'S TAIL HAS AN UNEQUAL UPPER LOBE. ITS BACKBONE EXTENDS INTO THE FIN. NURSE SHARKS ARE NOT STRONG SWIMMERS AND OFTEN REST ON THE BOTTOM. THEY DISPROVE THE MYTH THAT ALL SHARKS MUST KEEP MOVING OR THEY WILL DIE.

4 Shark Senses

Sharks have survived as a result of successful adaptations within their bodies. Often these features are different from those of other ocean inhabitants, such as the bony fishes, the whales, and the dolphins. However, often the need is the same, and through the evolutionary process small changes allow sharks to cope with changes in their environment, just as the bony fishes and marine mammals do.

Sound

> "ALL THE BETTER TO HEAR YOU WITH, MY DEAR."

Water is eight hundred times more dense than air. Humans seldom realize this because our ears are designed to catch sound

PROTECTED IN CHAIN MAIL, A DIVER IS FACE-TO-FACE WITH A REEF SHARK. IN ITS WATERY WORLD, THE SHARK NEEDS NONE OF THE SPECIAL EQUIPMENT THAT THE HUMAN MUST WEAR.

Shark body

2nd dorsal fin

dorsal fin

tail or
caudal fin

anal fin

pelvic fins

gill slits

pectoral fins

waves as they travel through "thin air." But sound travels faster and farther through the dense water. When you put your ear to a wall to hear into the next room, you are using the dense wall to transmit the sounds that are lost in the air.

Moreover, sharks hear not only through their ears, but with their whole body. They have a system of sound, or vibration, sensors known as the lateral line. Because external ears would drag against the water as they swim, sharks have internal ear structures. Specialized cells in pits, grooves, and canals on both sides of the shark's body contain hairs that vibrate, sending a signal to the shark's brain. Like our inner ears, which also control our sense of balance, the signals from the shark's sensors tell it which way is up, how fast it is moving, what currents are pushing it, and from what direction a sound is coming.

Sharks are also able to receive an image beyond their range of sight. They are continually receiving signals that tell where obstacles are, how the bottom is shaped, and more. They seem to use their inner ears for detecting noise that is far away, whereas the lateral line senses the vibrations closer to them.

The low-frequency beats of struggling fish attract sharks. Native islanders of Fiji have long used coconut rattles to lure sharks closer to their fishing lines. Modern sound recordings of these low frequencies have been played underwater. Researchers then monitor their attraction. Scientists are also searching for a frequency that will drive sharks away. More study is needed to find a repellent noise. This would be very useful protection since it could keep sharks away for long periods, unlike chemical repellents, which wash away.

Another sound that seems to attract sharks is the beat of helicopter blades. This is an uncomfortable thought for survivors hoping to be rescued as a helicopter hovers over the water.

Smell

"ALL THE BETTER TO SMELL YOU WITH, MY DEAR."

Sharks have been called "a swimming nose" because their sense of smell was thought to be so powerful. Blood in the water has always been thought to attract sharks. They seem to appear out of nowhere when injured prey is in the water. The part of a shark's brain that controls smell is exceptionally large, and sharks have been shown to detect substances as small as one part per million.

However, sharks use a variety of senses to locate the scene, not just the scent of blood itself. There are two openings, or nares, on the shark's snout. These are not connected to the mouth as a human's nose is, but are like two nostrils that allow water to pass in and out. The water travels over folds of receptor cells that increase the chemical signals from minute particles in the water. By sensing a stronger signal in one nostril than in the other, sharks are able to determine a sense of direction for the smell. Sharks are often seen moving their heads from side to side as they swim. This weaving back and forth helps them to home in on the source.

Land animals sense danger when they are downwind from a predator. In the same way, sharks swim against the current to follow a smell that is borne down current.

Electroreception

A shark sense that has only recently been discovered is that of electroreception—the ability to detect minute electrical discharges from biological sources, such as those that are produced when muscles contract. Modern methods of electronic measurement make it possible to detect the electrical impulses that exist unseen around us. For example, electrocardiographs are used regularly to record the heartbeats of human patients. The same kinds of electrical signals are now known to be picked up by sharks in organs known as the Ampullae of Lorenzini, named for the Italian scientist who found them. These are jelly-filled tubes located around the shark's head, just in front of the eyes.

Previously the function of these organs was thought to be associated with depth or temperature. Now scientists think that sharks can use them to sense the weak electrical signals that are generated by muscle activity, water flow, and perhaps even the magnetic field of the earth. Interpreting the lines of magnetism that exist around and under the sea would give sharks a kind of global positioning system without the need for satellites.

Sharks sometimes attack the metal propellers of boats or other metal objects. It is thought that they are responding to the electrical field that these items produce in seawater. Perhaps they mistake the impulse as similar to that produced by prey animals.

THE TINY PORES COVERING THE HEAD OF THIS BLUE SHARK ARE CALLED THE
AMPULLAE OF LORENZINI. THEY CAN DETECT MINUTE ELECTRICAL CHARGES GIVEN
OFF BY LIVING ANIMALS.

Taste

The shark's sense of taste comes from pits within the mouth.
Sharks will often sample items and then quickly reject them. For
example, a flounder of the Red Sea called the Moses sole
secretes a substance that totally repels sharks. Research has
been done to try to isolate this substance as a shark repellent.
On the other hand, some sharks, such as the tiger shark, eat

This tiger shark voids the contents of its stomach. This ability is useful because tiger sharks are known to eat anything, from beer cans to hubcaps.

almost anything. The kinds of objects found in their stomachs are often inedible and sometimes bizarre, such as license plates from cars. Sharks do seem to have a way of ridding themselves of the indigestible things they eat. Sharks in aquariums have been observed to empty their stomachs through their mouths by completely turning them inside out. They then bring their stomachs back into the body with no harm done.

5   Shark Ways

Whave only recently begun to understand the behavior of sharks. People often reduce things they don't understand to the simplest terms. If there is an element of danger, these things become myths, magic, demons, or monsters. Sharks are often reduced to such images: "A swimming nose," "the perfect eating machine," or "white death" are terms that reduce the shark to a simple and sometimes monstrous description.

But sharks are animals that are complex in their biology and behavior. They can be dangerous, but are no more terrible than "lions, and tigers, and bears." Somehow, the element of the unknown makes the shark appear to be a more frightening creature than it actually is. That is probably because sharks seem to have no reason for their actions. We can understand a mother bear protecting her cubs or a prowling tiger eating an unlucky native. But the thought of a shark "coming out of nowhere" remains terrifying to almost everyone.

PILOT FISH ACCOMPANY THE OCEANIC WHITE TIP SHARK, READY TO PICK UP CRUMBS FROM ITS FEEDING. SAILORS ONCE THOUGHT THESE FISH LED SHARKS TO THEIR PREY THE WAY PILOT BOATS LED THEIR SHIPS INTO HARBOR.

However, sharks, like all animals, behave in fairly pre-dictable and quite rational ways. We simply don't know what they are. They hunt, eat, and reproduce in a world that is out-side our view. The brief picture humans have from swimming with them in scuba gear or being dropped into their world in a shark cage only hints at how sharks spend their lives. As more and more people explore their world, some of these mysteries will be solved.

Shark Studies

One practice that has given a better picture of the shark's world is shark tagging. Scientists put tags on sharks in order to identify them as individuals. They are imbedded at the base of the dorsal fin, where the skin is thick, so as not to hurt the shark. The tags contain information such as where the shark was caught and on what date, as well as its sex and size. The sharks are then released carrying the tags. A reward is given to fishermen who notify scientists if they recapture one of these tagged sharks.

There are also shark tags designed to gather information while they are being dragged by a shark. These "data loggers" are minicomputers that record the location where the shark was tagged as well as such specific measurements as water temper-ature, depth, and salinity. It also gives a profile of where the shark went under the sea. Eventually, the tag is released (usual-ly when the attaching wire is corroded after a certain length of time) and floats to the surface. It then beams the stored data to a passing satellite, which in turn sends the data back to the sci-entists. The shark now swims free without dragging the tag, and since the tag does not need to be recovered, the scientists don't need to get their feet wet.

By attaching a tag to this lemon shark, scientists will be able to track its behavior. Modern tags are able to store information while the shark is submerged, then break free and send a signal to satellites as they pass overhead.

What We've Learned

Most of what we know about shark behavior has been derived from their brief encounters with fishermen, scuba divers, and attack victims. But as researchers record the results of their studies we gain a better understanding of the shark's world.

From studies such as shark tagging, we know that sharks often stay in one area. Some reef sharks were tracked to within ten minutes of being in the same spot at the same time of day, every day. One group of sharks that were observed over a three-year period remained in the same location. Most of their activity occurred during the night. This confirms what fishermen have believed for years. It also was found that some sharks gather together in schools for feeding, hunting, and mating purposes. In fact, sharks are sometimes called the "wolves of the sea."

Although some species cooperate in hunting together, individuals easily turn on one another as they compete to consume prey. Sometimes, a feeding frenzy develops, where feeding becomes so ferocious that the sharks accidentally bite one another. As these injured sharks weaken—and the sight, sound, and odor

SHARKS DRAW TOGETHER WHEN THEY SENSE PREY. SOMETIMES A "FEEDING FRENZY" OCCURS, AND THE OVER STIMULATED SHARKS ATTACK EACH OTHER.

WHEN SHARKS ACT LIKE BARKING DOGS

DIVERS ARE SOME-TIMES ABLE TO DRIVE SHARKS AWAY WITH THE USE OF A SPIKED CLUB CALLED A SHARK BILLY. BUT THIS IS NOT RELIABLE PROTECTION.

One of the observations that is most helpful in understanding the seemingly terrible behavior of sharks is that other animals behave in similar ways. Most other animals react by trying to exert their dominance if they feel threatened or cornered. Human swimmers have provoked many attacks, whether or not they intended to pose a threat.

Divers have seen that a shark behaves strangely just before an attack: The shark swims agitatedly; it arches its back and lowers its pectoral fins; then it makes a quick charge at the diver, which sometimes results in a bite or deep gash. It seems clear that this kind of attack is not associated with feeding, because usually the shark then moves away. It is more likely that the human has been perceived as a threat to the shark's territory. Just as a dog will raise its fur, snarl, and bark when threatened or challenged, a shark demonstrates a threat display. Under this circumstance, a shark's attack on a swimmer is just as "provoked" as a dog's attack on a mail carrier coming up to the front door with a package.

Unfortunately, a swimmer may not even realize he or she is blocking the shark's path. There is no warning bark, scent, or visual clue. The shark may sense the swimmer even in murky water and feel cornered. The swimmer remains oblivious to the whole underwater drama. The later report is likely to be that the shark "came out of nowhere and attacked me for no reason." And this again reinforces the old saying that "the only thing predictable about sharks is that they are unpredictable."

of blood, and thrashing motion excite the others—the injured members themselves become prey in a free-for-all of gluttony.

Mating and Reproduction

Bony Fish Reproduction. For any species to survive, it must successfully reproduce offspring. One way to ensure that some young will continue the species, is to produce so many babies that at least a few will have a chance to survive. Bony fish use this method successfully. Fish, such as the cod, release millions of eggs when they spawn. They mate by mixing sperm from the male with eggs from the female into the water.

Most fish will not live to maturity, but a few will escape predators and find enough food to grow up to repeat the process.

Shark Reproduction. Very little is known about the mating behavior of most sharks, but from observations by fishermen and divers and in aquariums, it is clear that sharks go through courtship and some complex mating rituals. For instance, the fins and backs of females often have bite marks during the mating season. The skin of the female blue shark is thickened along the neck to ensure that "love bites" will not do serious harm. It is three times thicker than the male's skin, and is also thicker than his teeth. When sharks finally mate, the male inserts a specialized organ called a clasper into the female.

Nature has devised different strategies for protecting the young while they are developing. In birds and reptiles the baby is kept safe inside a protective shell until it hatches. Often the parents also guard the nest, which further safeguards the young.

In mammals and many sharks the baby is kept inside the body of the mother until it is well developed. The male fertilizes the eggs, which are produced and kept inside the female's body.

A DIVER SHOWS THE SCARS FROM MATING BITES ON A FEMALE REEF SHARK. SHE IS IN AN EXHAUSTED TRANCE AFTER MATING.

This method of reproduction, called internal fertilization, gives the offspring a head start in life. Even ancient sharks used it as a successful method of reproduction.

There are three major ways that sharks reproduce: oviparous, ovoviviparous, and viviparous. Each method has evolved to give the species an advantage based on where it lives, how it feeds, and how it escapes predators.

Oviparous Reproduction: One way sharks reproduce is by laying eggs. This method is called oviparity. The embryo develops outside the mother, but is protected by a tough leathery shell. Sharks that use this method are usually bottom dwellers and live in an area where food is plentiful for their newly hatched offspring. The cat sharks, carpet sharks, and horned sharks lay eggs on the sea bottom or attach them with thin strings, or tendrils, to underwater plants or seaweed. Often beachcombers find the empty egg cases, known as mermaid's

THE EMBRYO IS CLEARLY SEEN IN THE EGG CASE OF THIS DOGFISH. THE FEMALE LAYS THE CASE, ALSO KNOWN AS A MERMAID'S PURSE, AND WRAPS IT WITH STRINGY TENDRILS OF KELP TO PROTECT THE EGG UNTIL IT HATCHES.

purses, washed ashore. These sharks may lay as many as twenty-five eggs. The eggs take nine to twelve months to hatch.

Ovoviviparous Reproduction: In other sharks the egg is kept inside the mother's body, where the embryo remains until it develops completely. The embryo is nourished by a yolk sac attached to its digestive system. This method is called ovoviviparous and is the most common among sharks. The babies are born well developed and ready to compete.

Ovoviviparous species usually produce fewer embryos than oviparous. The presence of a mother during the development stage ensures a greater survival rate than that for eggs left on their own. Some species, such as the spiny dogfish, have an exceptionally long period of gestation, or time until birth. Their

THIS SPINY DOGFISH, PROBABLY BORN PREMATURELY, STILL HAS THE YOLK SAC ATTACHED. IT RECEIVES NUTRITION FROM THIS SOURCE WHILE DEVELOPING WITHIN THE MOTHER.

FIRST COME, FIRST SERVED

S and tigers have a strange method of development. The embryos practice hunting within the mother! This cannibalism before birth is called oophagy.

Eggs are produced in the shark mother's two uterine tracts, one after another. As the first egg develops into an embryonic shark, it eats the next developing embryo. This continues until the birth of the two babies that have grown in each uterus. They grow strong feeding on their potential siblings. At birth, the young sand tiger sharks are forty inches (100 cm) in length, and completely ready to hunt on their own.

pregnancy lasts twenty-four months! Aside from dogfish, frill sharks, tiger sharks, great white sharks, and some nurse sharks use this method.

Viviparous Reproduction: In a manner that is similar to human and mammal development, some sharks have a placenta. This is tissue that connects the embryo with its mother, and provides the developing baby with oxygen and nutrients. The placenta also removes the embryo's waste products. Hammerheads, the whalers, and blue sharks use this method.

THE BODY OF THIS PREGNANT SAND TIGER SHARK IS VERY DISTENDED. IT WILL GIVE BIRTH TO WELL-DEVELOPED YOUNG.

A Gallery of Sharks

6

"KNUT HAD BEEN SQUATTING THERE, WASHING HIS PANTS IN
THE SWELL, AND WHEN HE LOOKED UP FOR A MOMENT HE WAS
STARING STRAIGHT INTO THE BIGGEST AND UGLIEST FACE ANY
OF US HAD EVER SEEN IN THE WHOLE OF OUR LIVES."

Kon-Tiki, Thor Heyerdahl, about a whale shark

The Big

Whale Shark. At close to forty feet (15 m), the whale shark is the largest fish in the ocean. The great whales are bigger, but they are mammals, not fish. Fortunately the whale shark is of no danger to humans, since it hunts only small fishes and plankton. It is very much like the great baleen whales in size and behavior. It keeps its huge mouth open to allow water to pass through its gill rakers—fine strainerlike structures on the inner side of the gills— as it swims and strains the small organisms from the water. Whale sharks also engulf whole schools of small fish. They look

THE WHALE SHARK IS OFTEN CALLED A GENTLE GIANT.
ITS HUGE FORM IS OF LITTLE DANGER TO HUMANS.

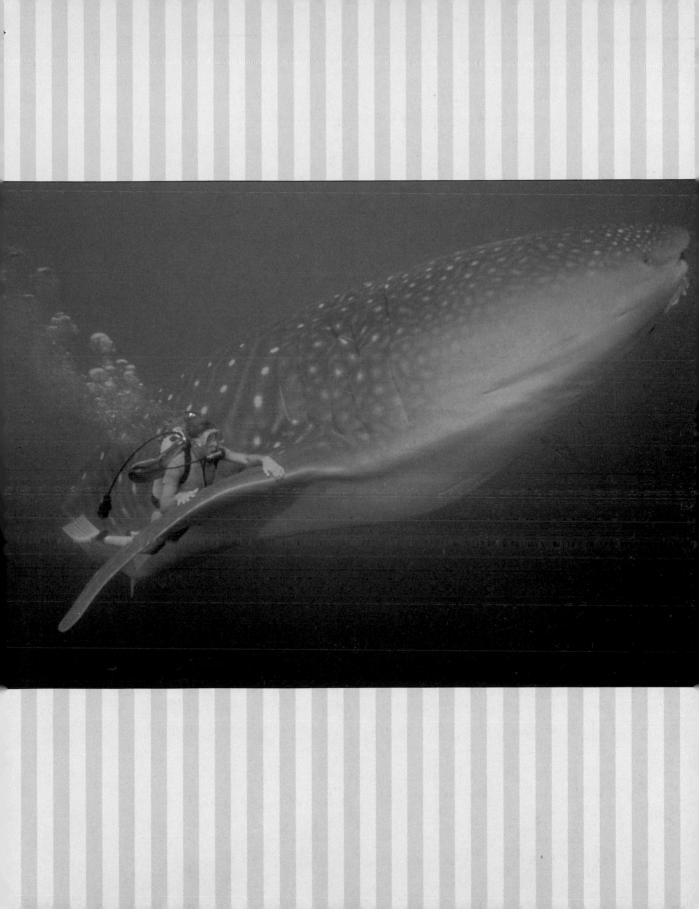

for schools that are tightly balled up, perhaps trying to escape other predators. When a whale shark finds a school of fish, it rises vertically out of the water to drain the water volume out of its mouth, then drops back into the ocean next to the school. Water and fish rush into the whale shark's mouth.

Whale sharks are found in warm waters throughout the world. They are known to gather in certain areas, perhaps when breeding or giving birth. They are very docile and will actually allow divers to "hitch a ride" on their backs. This has lead to great interest from tourists who want to see these giant fish up close.

The whale shark is in the same order as the nurse shark, the highly camouflaged wobbegong, and all of the other carpet sharks. However, its shape is different from the rest of this bottom-dwelling group. The whale shark's shape is more typical of the mackerel sharks and the requiem sharks but, unlike those two species, its large mouth is at the front of the body rather than underslung. This characteristic helps put it into the carpet shark group.

Whale sharks were once thought to be egg layers, but pregnant females have been caught containing hundreds of live young ready to be born.

Basking Shark. The second-largest shark is the basking shark. It is named for its behavior of quietly laying in the surface waters of cooler oceans to bask in the sun. This shark is a slow swimmer that cruises through plankton-rich waters and strains out small crustaceans, fish eggs, and other organisms in the same manner as the great baleen whales and the whale shark. It passes up to 2,000 tons of water through its gill rakers every hour.

Basking sharks have long been hunted for their oil, meat, and fins. Their enormous livers may weigh up to one ton and hold four hundred gallons (1,500 l) of oil. Shark oil was burned for light, the same as whale oil, in the days before electricity. It is still used as a source of vitamin A in medicinal products.

Recent surveys show that the population of basking sharks has been severely reduced and is in need of protection. Even in areas where fishing is restricted, the numbers are still declining. It may be that these animals are so dependent on water quality

THE BASKING SHARK FEEDS ON TINY PLANKTON. AS A GRAZER, IT REACHES A GIANT SIZE, MUCH LIKE THE ELEPHANTS AND OTHER GRAZING MAMMALS ON LAND.

that the slightest change can be very harmful. To be sure, we already know that the planktonic organisms on which they feed are greatly affected by water pollution. The loss of basking sharks may indicate greater changes that will eventually affect other ocean-dwelling species.

No embryos have been found within the few females that have been examined by fishermen over the years. It is therefore thought that the females may go into deep water to give birth and stay there for perhaps up to two or more years while the baby sharks develop. But as is true of many sharks, scientists do not know any actual details. There is some thought that basking sharks may hibernate in deep water. They may shed their gill rakers and rest before growing new ones. Dr. Eugenie Clark, who has been studying sharks all her life, examined a dead basking shark that had an empty stomach and no gill rakers. Tiny gill rakers were growing, as if they were a new set coming in.

Basking sharks have measured thirty feet (9 m). The animals seem slow and sluggish, but have been reported to leap completely out of the water. This behavior, which is amazing for heavy animals such as the great whales or basking sharks, may be a way of freeing themselves of parasites or of communicating by means of the great crash they make as they fall back into the water.

Megamouth. In 1976 U.S. Navy personnel found a strange and totally unknown shark entangled in equipment that was being pulled up from a depth of five hundred feet (150 m). Scientists recognized this fish as a new species. It was a male, 14.5 feet (4.8 m) long, weighing 1,653 pounds (750 kg). It had a huge mouth, and from its stomach contents, it was clearly a plankton feeder. It was quickly called megamouth. The mouth was lined with luminescent, or glowing, tissue that probably attracts deep-sea shrimp. The fact that this fish had never before

SEA SERPENTS

In the 1960s, an expert in Boston reported that a strange new creature had washed ashore—the Situate Sea Serpent. He claimed it had the head of a camel, the neck of a giraffe, and the body of a whale. "Anyone who calls this a shark must be crazy," he said to the press. And so it seemed—until the missing pieces were fitted back into place.

Stories of sea serpents often arise as the result of finding a basking shark body washed ashore. The gills and gill rakers make up almost a complete ring just behind the fish's head. The gills are loosely supported and easily break off the body when a basking shark dies and begins to decompose. As the dead body is banged about in the surf, the gills along with the lower jaw break off. This leaves a long neck exposed on a massive body.

THE MEGAMOUTH SHARK WAS UNKNOWN UNTIL THE LATE TWENTIETH CENTURY.
WHAT OTHER SEA ANIMALS ARE YET TO BE DISCOVERED?

been seen adds to the evidence that it is a resident of the deep ocean. Many fish and invertebrates of that region have luminescent organs that produce light, or bioluminescence, to attract prey. Megamouth has a weak muscle structure and is a slow swimmer.

Since 1976, more than eleven specimens have been found. One was kept alive, tagged, and released. Scientists are just beginning to learn about the creatures that live in the dark world of the deep sea. That this shark remained undiscovered until recently leads to speculation whether other strange sharks may inhabit that world.

The Strange

Goblin Shark. A rare shark whose closest relatives were believed to be extinct for 100 million years was caught off the coast of Japan in the later 1890s. Called the goblin shark, this fish has since been taken in water more than 1,150 feet (350 m) deep near Portugal, India, and Australia. The maximum size known is 12.5 feet (4 m).

The goblin shark's bizarre snout is covered with the Ampullae of Lorenzini and probably helps the fish detect the weak electrical charges of its prey. This adaptation looks as if it were added on.

Cookie-cutter Shark. This shark, which only grows up to twenty inches (50 cm), has giant teeth compared to its body size. Proportionally, they are bigger than even the great whites. And the cookie-cutter shark uses these teeth to attack whales!

Cookie-cutter sharks live in deep water and are the most brilliant of the bioluminescent sharks. Their common name, cookie-cutter, is appropriate. The shark gouges perfectly round, bite-sized chunks out of a whale's skin. To bite, the shark presses its lips against the side of the whale or other large animal and

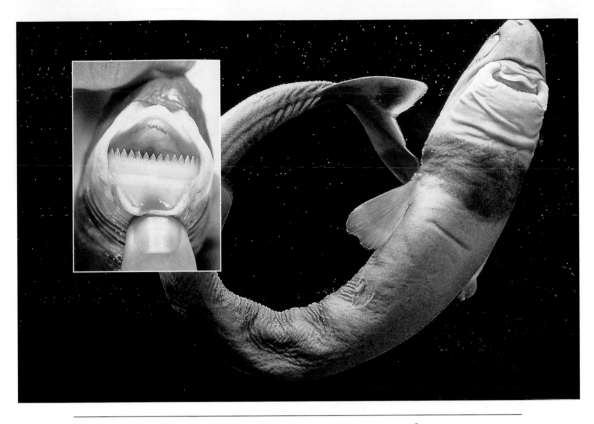

THE COOKIE CUTTER SHARK IS A SMALL, BUT AMBITIOUS HUNTER. IT TAKES PERFECTLY ROUND BITES OUT OF ANIMALS MANY TIMES ITS SIZE.

sucks the flesh into its mouth. Then its sharp teeth sink in, and the shark twists its whole body, cutting out a bite about the size of a golf ball.

It was not until the feeding technique of the cookie-cutter shark was learned that the little round holes on the sides of tuna, whales, and other sharks could be explained. The U.S. Navy even found holes in the rubber coverings on submarines.

Pygmy Shark. Another bioluminescent shark, the pygmy shark, lives at a depth of about 1,600 feet (490 m) by day and comes closer to the surface at night. It is the smallest known shark. Fully mature sharks that were caught measured less than five inches (12 cm).

This shark is found in deep waters around the world, although none have been caught near North America. It has a spine in front of the first dorsal fin. Other sharks with spines have them in front of both dorsals.

Spiny Dogfish. This small shark is a fish of cold water. Spiny dogfish may be the most abundant sharks in the sea. In fact, they are so abundant that fishermen sometimes have to try not to catch them when they are fishing for more valuable species. However, spiny dogfish are fished in their own right as well. Once, when cod and haddock were abundant, spiny dogfish were used only for fertilizer or burned as fuel. Now that other fisheries have been depleted, spiny dogfish are used to supply the market for "fish and chips," a popular dish in Great Britain. Spiny dogfish are sometimes disguised under the name of "rock salmon" to give it more appeal.

The body form and organs of the spiny dogfish are typical

SPINY DOGFISH HAVE SPINES AT THE BASE OF EACH DORSAL FIN. THEY CAN GIVE FISHERMEN A NASTY STAB WOUND.

enough of sharks in general for this shark to be used for dissection in biology classes all over the world. A spine in front of each dorsal fin gives this shark part of its common name, spiny. Those spines help protect it from predators and have given many fishermen a nasty prick. The spines have some venom in them, which can make the wound far more serious than the stab of the spine itself. While the wounds have never been known to cause the death of a human, reactions to the venom have caused sickness and severe pain.

The abundance of dogfish may be dwindling. Although they can live for up to seventy years, it takes females twenty to twenty-five years to reach maturity. And the embryos take two years to develop. This is more than twice as long as it takes humans!

The Deadly

Great White Shark. No book on sharks would be complete without the great white. It is known by different names around the world. In Australia it is called the white pointer and sometimes white death. Recent authors simply call it the white shark. But even adding "great" may not do it full justice.

The great white is a wide-ranging species that is at home in tropical and colder waters worldwide. The movie *Jaws* made it a celebrity, but very little is known about its life history, even though it is implicated in a large percentage of shark attacks on humans. Off the coast of California great whites have attacked humans an average of 1.3 times per year.

Great whites are as formidable as any creature in the sea. The largest size of the great white is disputed, although reliable measurements approach twenty feet (6 m) and over two tons. Reports of great whites more than thirty feet (10 m) long and weighing more than seven thousand pounds (3,175 kg) exist but may not be accurate. It is simply difficult to weigh or even measure an animal that large, so reports are sometimes unreliable.

The great white is a graceful swimmer with a streamlined body. Its speed is probably used for a sudden surprise attack on its prey. The top of the great white is a dull gray that blends into the haze of deeper water when viewed from above. The white underside, from which it gets its name, blends into the surface light when viewed from below. Fighter planes are often painted in this color pattern to minimize their visibility.

THE GREAT WHITE SHARK IS PURE WHITE ON THE UNDERSIDE AND GRAY ABOVE. IN THE OPEN OCEAN, THIS IS GOOD CAMOUFLAGE. IT RANGES THROUGHOUT ALL BUT THE COLDEST OCEANS.

A seal swimming up to the surface to breathe, and relying mostly on sight to sense its surroundings, would be unaware of a great white below. On the other hand, the shark senses the seal's movements through its lateral line, or sees the outline silhouetted against the surface light. A few sweeps of the powerful tail, and the massive body rockets upward. The great mouth opens and the seal is borne out of the water, flailing against rows of sharp and serrated teeth. The shark releases the seal and circles the scene while the crippled animal weakens. Once the seal loses strength from this initial massive attack, the great white returns to bite and consume its meal.

This feeding strategy may account for some remarkable rescues of human victims. After an initial strike, great whites have backed off, ignoring other swimmers. This action allowed enough time for the victims to be pulled from the water—and the jaws of death. The great white may have been simply waiting for the victim to bleed to death and had no interest in anything else. However, this does not diminish the heroism of rescuers who faced these horrible scenes to save companions.

Hammerhead Shark. The great flat head of this shark clearly must have a purpose. But what? A number of possibilities have been suggested to account for this seemingly unwieldy feature. One theory is that the flattened head serves as a wing that gives additional lift to that of the pectoral fins. While this makes some sense, other sharks seem to get along without such a strange head.

As scientists come to better understand the electrical receptor sensing of sharks they now believe that this head may serve as a kind of mine sweeper or metal detector, helping hammerheads find their favorite prey—bottom-dwelling fish and rays. These creatures hide by burying themselves in the sand and become virtually invisible. Their large heads are covered with Ampullae of Lorenzini. By sweeping their heads back and forth,

HAMMERHEAD SHARKS MAY LOOK AWKWARD AND BIZARRE, BUT THEY ARE FIERCE PREDATORS AND CAN BE DANGEROUS TO HUMANS.

hammerheads are able to detect the electrical signals of fish hiding in the sand. Hammerheads can be quite large and have been responsible for attacks on humans. The great hammerhead reaches twenty feet (6 m).

Other members of this family of nine species are the small bonnethead and the scalloped hammerhead. Scalloped hammerheads are known to congregate in large schools in specific locations. For example, in Mexico's Sea of Cortés there is a seamount, an undersea mountain sometimes close to the surface, that attracts hammerheads. No one knows what attracts them, but hundreds of hammerheads mill around the seamount. It is unusual for large predators to group together. Researchers are trying to learn if this gathering is part of a migration pattern or perhaps a ritual in the mating process. This area, which was chanced upon by scuba divers, only suggests that these and perhaps other species may come together in other remote parts of the ocean. Perhaps tagging studies will help form a picture of the hammerhead's mysterious world.

Tiger Shark. Even if it did not have the vertical stripes that gave it its name, this shark would probably be called tiger for its ferocity and reputation as a man-eater. Tiger sharks are omnivores. They will eat anything, and are famous for the amazing things that have been found in their stomachs: coal, boat cushions, unopened cans of tuna, suits of armor, and birds. As omnivores, tiger sharks have been known to include humans in their diet. Tiger sharks have distinctive teeth that are sickle-shaped with serrated edges. They can cut into a wide variety of materials. Sea turtles are often seen missing a flipper or with a crescent-shaped bite right through the shell.

Tiger sharks are found all over the world in warm coastal waters. They usually stay offshore during the day but come into very shallow water at night to feed. One tiger shark was photographed at a depth of 1,000 feet (300 m).

The role of sharks as predators that cull out the weakest and less fit is clear from the observations of Wesley Strong, a researcher for the Cousteau Society. He watched more than one hundred attacks by tiger sharks on fledgling albatrosses that were leaving their nests. Often young albatrosses could make only short flights in their first attempts. As they landed in the water to rest, the tiger sharks would pull them below the surface. Strong estimated that ten percent of the baby birds were lost from the rookery. The tiger sharks were weeding out the weak, leaving the stronger birds to survive.

The tiger shark is the only requiem shark that has ovoviviparous reproduction. Females can have ten to eighty-two babies, or pups, in a litter after a gestation period of twelve to thirteen months.

Bull Shark. The bull shark possesses a most dangerous trait. It inhabits areas that people often share, such as lakes and rivers. The bull is also a shark of many names. It was often named after the river or lake in which it was commonly found and then thought to be separate species. However, scientists now know this to be a single species. The bull shark's range is worldwide. For instance, the Nicaragua shark, Zambezi shark, freshwater whaler (in Australia), and Ganges shark are all names for the same fish. Once thought to be a landlocked species in Lake Nicaragua, bull sharks are now known to travel up the San Juan River from the Caribbean. Bull sharks can travel long distances up rivers—some have been found 2,300 miles (3,700 km) up the Amazon.

The bull shark can be confused with any of the requiem sharks. It is of "typical" shark size and shape, with a high dorsal fin set a bit forward on a broad back. This bull-like appearance is difficult to distinguish, which is why the bull shark is often mistaken in an attack. In some cases, this mistaken identity is the reason bull sharks are blamed for attacks that others may have committed; and in other cases, great whites or tigers are blamed for the work of bull sharks. In any case, bull sharks are extremely dangerous, and particularly so when they are around highly populated rivers and lakes.

The maximum size of a bull shark is about eleven feet (3.3 m) and it can weigh 670 pounds (304 kg). It has a heavy body and broad pectoral fins with pointed tips. Juveniles have black tips.

Bull sharks prey on their cousins the sandbar sharks, and on other fish. Often called sluggish and scavengers, bulls may be the most frequent killers of humans, simply because they come closest to the shallow coastal bays, inlets, and rivers where humans are most often in the water.

THE BULL SHARK TESTS THE CAGE OF AN UNDERWATER PHOTOGRAPHER. ITS RANGE OFTEN BRINGS IT CLOSE TO HUMANS, MAKING IT ONE OF THE MOST DANGEROUS SHARKS.

Oceanic Whitetip. Fortunately, the oceanic whitetip shark lives offshore, away from people. Otherwise, it might be far more famous as a man-eater. Named for its broad fins tipped in white, this large shark is fearless and aggressive. Whitetips grow to a length of up to thirteen feet (4 m). It is thought that the oceanic whitetip has been responsible for terrible attacks on the victims of sea disasters. The tales of sailors cast into the water due to wartime engagements are horrible. Oceanic whitetips are the likely culprits. This is based on some factual identification and also the fact that they appear in large numbers whenever any attraction is in the waters of the open sea.

7 Sharks and Us

It is impossible to discuss sharks without turning the focus to the stories of their attacks on people. There are some completely harmless sharks with interesting stories about how and where they live. However, it is the fascination that people have for the gruesomeness of shark attacks that drives any conversation about these creatures.

International Shark Attack File

Records of shark attacks from the mid-1500s to the present are kept in the International Shark Attack File (ISAF). These reports have been verified and entered into a database that is administered by the American Elasmobranch Society and the Florida

A BLUE SHARK BITES ON A CHAIN MAIL SUIT. AS MORE HUMANS ENTER THE SHARK'S DOMAIN, MORE INTERACTIONS WILL TAKE PLACE AND BOTH SPECIES WILL NEED PROTECTION.

Museum of Natural History at the University of Florida in Gainesville. From this, scientists try to make sense of the many reports of shark attacks and evaluate factors that might help us understand, and perhaps prevent them. For instance, do sharks really attack people who wear yellow bathing suits, as divers suspect? If the records actually showed that a larger number of the recorded attacks were on those yellow-suited bathers, sales for that color swimsuit would likely drop.

Provoked Attacks. The International Shark Attack File separates attacks into two categories. One is provoked, where humans, often unintentionally, make contact with the shark. For example, swimmers or divers who grab the tail of supposedly harmless sharks find out that "harmless" is a relative term. The nurse shark is usually considered harmless. It is a small-mouthed shark, but it still has teeth: And even though the teeth are small, they can take a chunk of flesh that leaves a serious wound.

Just about any shark attack is likely to take place away from medical care. This is because the kind of recreation that puts people in contact with sharks is almost always at a remote beach, or from a boat. The route to a hospital is usually not easy, or close.

Many fatal shark attacks are caused by small sharks that do minimal damage. (Minimal, as compared with what might happen in an automobile accident.) Nevertheless, people die from loss of blood or shock before they can get the necessary medical attention.

Unprovoked Attacks. It is the unprovoked attacks that are the greatest threat to humans. These occur without human provocation—that is, "the shark started it." Many times the shark also finishes it. Fortunately, however, most of these attacks are not the case of a terrible predator out to eat humans.

The ISAF classifies many attacks as "hit and run." These are attacks that may surprise bathers close to shore, at a depth of

THE GREAT WHITE SHARK OFTEN STRIKES ITS PREY WITH A SLASHING CHARGE. IT
THEN CIRCLES WHILE THE VICTIM BLEEDS AND WEAKENS.

less than six feet (2 m). This, of course, is the most popular depth
for people to play in the surf. Usually the wounds from this kind
of attack are not severe. Typically, the shark quickly grabs and
releases the lower leg or hand. The shark does not return to
attack again.

It is thought that this type of "hit and run" attack occurs
because the shark mistakes the splash of the arms and legs for
small fishes that it had been pursuing. Another possibility is that

the shark perceives the human's body as a threat to its territory or dominance. Of course the human is not aware of this. Divers who have observed these kinds of attacks underwater report that the shark seems to feel it is being cornered and attacks in self-defense.

Within the unprovoked attack category, the ISAF lists other types of attacks that have serious consequences. The sneak attack is used to define an attack that seems to come out of nowhere. A violent and unexpected first bite can be followed by repeated attacks in which the victim may actually be eaten. A sneak attack is the method of choice for the great white, which inflicts so much damage on its first rush that the victim is doomed instantly.

"Bump and bite" describes another terrible type of shark attack. When large sharks are able to approach an object easily, as they can an injured sea creature—and most humans swim like injured sea creatures—they are likely to test the condition and sense the object before committing to a bite. Human victims are usually in deeper water and have reported first feeling a bump while the shark passed. For the lucky ones, the shark probably sensed something distasteful or threatening during the bump and these people likely came away with only an abrasion from the rough skin. Others who were less lucky, and perhaps were dealing with a hungrier shark, have had the shark circle and repeat the attack.

In both the sneak as well as the bump and bite attacks, the intent of the shark seems to be to attack the victim as prey. It is likely that this is a case of mistaken identity. A human surfer may look too much like a sea lion to pass up, or a swimmer who thinks he or she is doing the perfect breaststroke looks like an injured turtle with its flippers flopping. In either case, the mistaken identity defense does the victim no good, and depending on its state of hunger, the shark may make a meal of this unusual-tasting critter.

Sharks As Food

Sharks have been labeled killers and at times have been hunted as if to rid the seas of vermin. Other times they have been hunted because killing them is seen as a macho symbol of human dominance over a dangerous animal. Certainly primitive peoples showed their bravery and prowess by displaying the teeth, claws, and skins of their prey. Strength was supposed to have come from the animals they killed.

However, in today's world such symbols of prowess seem misplaced, especially because modern methods reduce the amount of real bravery necessary to accomplish a kill. Sharks have been slaughtered for the sake of sport, which some have blamed on the near panic caused by the movie *Jaws*. But such sport existed long before the movie. Such unnecessary and wanton kills may be a remnant of humankind's prehistoric mind. Recently, however, the public mind-set is far more protective and sensitive to shark conservation than ever before.

Sharks need protection more from commercial fishing than random acts of wanton cruelty. Sharks have become an important food source. Overfishing for bony fish has depleted stocks of important food fish such as cod and haddock, but shark populations are far more vulnerable. Bony fish reproduce millions of offspring, which grow to maturity quickly. If the conditions are corrected, the fishery can recover in a relatively short time. On the other hand, sharks take a long time to grow to maturity, they have a long gestation period, and they produce a small number of offspring—sometimes as few as two and never more than one hundred. Once a population of sharks is overfished, it may never recover, even if fishing is stopped.

Shark meat is now commonly sold in fish markets throughout the United States. People of many countries eat shark and its popularity continues to increase. Mako is one of the most popular, and compares well with swordfish for broiled and grilled steaks.

In Asia, a long tradition of preparing a gourmet dish, shark fin soup, persists in restaurants. The soup commands such high prices that sharks are fished only for the fins. Since the fins bring such a high price, fishermen cut the fins from the shark and toss the still-alive shark back overboard. They do not want to fill their boats with the almost worthless bodies. They want only the valuable fins, which need no refrigeration or special treatment other

THE FINS OF SHARKS ARE USED FOR EXOTIC ASIAN SOUPS AND COMMAND HIGH PRICES. WHEN SHARKS ARE CAUGHT ONLY FOR THEIR FINS, IT IS A WASTEFUL FISHING PRACTICE.

than drying in the sun. The finless shark is doomed to die a slow death. This wasteful and inhumane practice has been condemned by nations around the world. Laws are now in place that hopefully will discourage finning even in the most remote areas.

As wasteful as finning is, it accounts for far less destruction of sharks than a method of catching fish called drift netting. Floating gill nets, so called because large fish that swim into them are caught around their gills, can be up to thirty miles (50 km) long. They catch every creature that happens to swim in, including turtles and marine mammals. Fishermen only take the higher-prized fish and discard the rest. This is wasteful, but even more so because sometimes these nets are lost. They continue to drift unattended, catching and killing sea animals for years. These ghost nets have caused enough damage so that regulations are being established to outlaw their use.

Protecting Sharks

Sharks are now being protected. So many great whites were taken by sport fisherman and thrill seekers that they soon became scarce. Between 1970 and 1993, surveys were done that showed shark populations had declined by more than 75 percent. As a result, the Fishery Management Plan for Sharks of the Atlantic Ocean was established. The plan covers thirty-nine species of sharks, but many still remain unprotected. Tagging studies also showed that great whites were declining. Now the great white is protected off California, South Africa, and part of Australia.

But why should anyone protect sharks, which are known to kill humans? The same can be asked about tigers. For one thing, both the great white and the tiger are magnificent creatures. To many people, the world would be a less interesting place if they were gone. More important, however, the tiger in the jungle and the great white in the ocean are the top predators. Without predators, the balance of the natural world is disrupted. Predators control overpopulation and remove the weakest and less fit members. This results in a stronger population of the prey species. For example, in the northeastern United States predators such as wolves have been removed, leaving populations of deer to overrun their habitat and often die from starvation.

Living with Sharks

How can people and sharks live together? People are able to live with dangers such as plane crashes, automobile accidents, and other threats once they understand the danger and take measures to minimize the risk. Can the danger from sharks be prevented? In many ways, the answer is yes. The more we know about their behavior, the better we can predict and even prevent attacks on people.

Preventive Measures. The best way to avoid a shark attack is simply to stay out of the water. This is virtually 100 percent effective. Although . . . there is the case of the tourist who reached into his bag for the carved shark statue that he had brought back as a gift from the South Pacific. The carving had real shark teeth imbedded in the jaws, and the tourist cut his finger as he groped among his clothing. So even being miles from the ocean is not a complete guarantee.

In any event, many measures are in place that allow sharks and people to coexist. Sometimes humans do have to protect themselves and eliminate sharks from some areas, but perhaps methods to repel them would be effective enough without the need to kill them.

The military has tried to find repellents that will protect

sailors and fliers when they are cast into the sea. During World War II, for example, military personnel were often in shark-infested waters and the fear of being attacked by sharks was as frightening to pilots as the fear of being shot down. The U.S. Navy developed a chemical packet called Shark Chaser that was issued as part of their survival kit. Shark Chaser was a dye mixed with the chemical copper acetate. Later tests showed that although Shark Chaser was a great name, it was a useless product. It had virtually no effect on sharks. In fact, in some instances they ate the canister. However, it gave the pilots a sense of safety to have it with them.

Scientists know of one shark repellent that really works. In the Red Sea there is a flatfish called the Moses sole. It has been observed that when a shark begins to bite this fish it immediately stops and flees. Scientists have found that the Moses sole produces a chemical in a milky white fluid that protects it from

The Moses sole has a protection besides its excellent camouflage. It produces a chemical in its mucus so repellent to sharks that they will stop an attack in mid-bite.

sharks. Many attempts have been made to refine this chemical and apply its use to humans. So far these efforts have been unsuccessful, because the chemical repellent is too easily washed away.

Some areas, such as South Africa, have beautiful beaches, a large human population, and lots of dangerous sharks. An expensive but effective way to use a beach safely is to create fenced-in swimming areas. However, entire coastlines cannot be completely fenced.

Beaches of Australia, South Africa, and South America use another technique that is less expensive than complete fencing but effective nonetheless. Nets are put up offshore from popular beaches and checked every day. In this way, the population of potentially dangerous sharks is reduced, lessening the chances of an encounter.

Other methods of keeping sharks away have been tried; few have worked well. A "bubble curtain" was thought to have promise. With this method, bubbles are pumped through holes in a pipe to form a wall. However, few sharks are deterred by it. Electric fields were also thought to be a possible shark deterrent. These created a barrier and shocked sharks as they passed through them, perhaps scaring them from the area. Unfortunately, this system is difficult to use in salt water and extremely expensive.

Portable Protective Devices. The best methods for preventing shark attacks are the use of physical barriers such as fencing and meshing, because they keep sharks and people from coming in contact with one another. However, not all areas are netted or fenced. Portable underwater devices have been developed that can give swimmers and divers some protection from sharks.

Scuba divers often use a club, or "shark billy," to ward off aggressive sharks. Any hard object can be effective, including a

SOME SOUTH AFRICAN BEACHES ARE PROTECTED BY ANTI-SHARK NETTING TO PROTECT SWIMMERS.

speargun, camera housing, or even a fist. However, a club is useful only to ward off sharks and probably will not work against a large shark intent on a serious attack. Plus, it is useful only for divers who wear masks and make good visual contact with the shark.

Divers can also use "bang sticks," which are like underwater shotguns without a barrel. They are also called powersticks and are designed to fire a shotgun shell on contact. This explosive shot can kill even large sharks. In the past, divers killed sharks for sport when no danger was present. The diving community now discourages this practice.

The U.S. Navy has developed other antishark devices to protect their frogmen. One is a dart that injects carbon dioxide gas into the shark's body cavity, causing it to inflate or even explode. An electric stungun, called a shark-tazer, may have some possibilities as a weapon as well.

All of these devices may be useful for personal protection underwater but they are of little help to the majority of shark attack victims, who never see their attacker. People who scuba dive for abalone, a highly prized shellfish, in California are perhaps the most exposed. That is because they dive in the same waters where great whites hunt for elephant seals. The divers' chances of attack are so great that when they dive, they stay inside mobile shark cages, which are boxes constructed of metal bars. Underwater photographers use shark cages regularly to get pictures of dangerous sharks like the great white. Some of these photographers have come to know the great white so well that they are able to tell whether the shark is a threat or not. Although it may be risky, they feel comfortable leaving the cage. Experienced guides and some native people are able to do the same thing around dangerous land animals. With the proper experience and knowledge, sharks can become more predictable.

IN THE REALM OF THE SHARK, HUMANS MUST RELY ON MAN-MADE PROTECTION. THIS SHARK CAGE SEEMS FRAGILE COMPARED TO THE MASSIVE GREAT WHITE.

Recent Developments. The Natal Sharks Board, an organization that has been studying the problem of shark attacks in South Africa for many years, has developed a device that may provide real protection against attack. Divers can wear devices called SharkPODs, which continually emit an electrical field that deters sharks. The shark's Ampullae of Lorenzini pick up this electrical signal, which is weak by human standards but strong enough to cause discomfort to a sensitive shark.

Statistics—Help or Hindrance?

International Shark Attack File (ISAF) records show trends that may give clues as to why sharks attack. These records form the data, or statistics about shark attacks. They show information such as which sharks attack the most, what time of day most attacks occur, and what people are doing when they are attacked.

While the information in the ISAF database may give some good information, it may also lead us to incorrect conclusions. For instance, there was a theory that sharks never attacked humans in water that was colder than 72 degrees Fahrenheit (22°C). This theory was based on the fact that there were no

In many parts of the world shark attacks go completely unreported. Many sharks inhabit the poorest areas of the world—tropical islands and parts of India and Asia—where there are few hospitals to help the victims, and poor communication systems for reporting attacks. Many people in these areas simply think of shark attacks as common accidents.

HOW TO AVOID A SHARK ATTACK

- Know which are the dangerous sharks and where they live. Some are real man-eaters, and if there is any chance of a great white, tiger, bull, hammerhead, or other known killer nearby, take the best precaution—get out of the water.

- Avoid behaviors that attract sharks. Sharks are known to be drawn to distress signals. They may be encouraged to attack if you are engaging in behavior that is like that of their normal prey. Swim smoothly and without splashy motions.

- Avoid wearing bright or flashy clothes or jewelry in the water. Sharks are attracted to the flash of swimming fish.

- Do not stay in the water if you are bleeding. Sharks are drawn to the smell of blood.

- Do not stay near injured or struggling fish. The vibrations that they cause will bring sharks

- Do not swim with dogs; their swimming motion, the dog paddle, may attract sharks.

- Be aware of the most dangerous times. Sharks are far more active at night, so avoid swimming at dusk or at night.

- Avoid the most dangerous places. If a shark attack has occurred in an area before, stay away. Just as lightning will strike in the same place, sharks have preferred hunting grounds.

reports of humans being attacked in water colder than that temperature. According to the statistics it was safe to swim in the cold waters of the world. However, people do not like to swim in cold water. Therefore, the lack of shark attacks in cold water had more to do with there being fewer swimmers to attack than with the sharks not attacking in those waters. It is now clear that those early statistics gave the wrong picture.

The statistics are clear about one fact. The chance of shark attack is greater the closer one is to people-eating sharks. As simple as it sounds, all the statistics add up to that obvious fact. Some theories make it sound as if shark attacks are unusual and only happen because the human made some mistake—as if the shark didn't mean it or wouldn't have attacked if the human had behaved differently. This is incorrect. Many sharks are dangerous animals and will attack, and sometimes eat, human beings.

It is better to understand this fact and take precautions than to deny the danger. The danger of air travel is understood, and people take extra precautions to keep themselves reasonably safe.

Save the Sharks

Conservation efforts have helped many species that were near extinction. Elephants and whales have recovered under international protection from hunting. Also, efforts are being made to preserve entire ecosystems, or areas where animals live, such as rain forests and reefs.

Sharks may be one of the most threatened sea creatures in the world. The behavior and adaptations that helped them evolve successfully over four hundred million years may give them little chance in today's world. Overfishing is causing many shark species to decline, perhaps in some cases to a point of no return. Their slow rate of reproduction may limit a shark species' ability to make a comeback even when fishing is banned. Our knowledge of habitats, migratory routes, breeding sites, and nursery grounds is minimal. It is almost impossible to develop plans for shark conservation until we understand the whole life history. For example, preventing fishing for adult sharks in one area while leaving nursery areas unprotected may do no good at all. The governments of many countries around the world are getting together to develop laws to conserve fisheries.

People are learning more about sharks and as a result can begin to respect them as wonderful creatures that have a predator's role in the oceans. This does not mean that humans do not have to be careful or that sharks are harmless. With caution and understanding, we can live together with a controlled level of risk.

It is clear that sharks are more at risk than humans. Sharks are hunted for their oil, skin, meat, fins, cartilage, and teeth. Consumer education—understanding that fishermen catch what people will buy—has helped reduce the loss of dolphins and whales. Our efforts to buy only "dolphin safe" tuna has prevented the killing of many of the dolphins caught in huge nets along with tuna. The United Nations has banned the use of drift nets on the high seas. These nets caught millions of tons of sharks and other fish as by-catch, or the catch made when fishing for something else.

It is hoped that conservation measures and cooperation between international fishermen will preserve sharks and their habitats. But it is too early to tell. Global problems may override the best efforts of conservationists. Atmospheric gases from pollution may be causing an increase in the average temperature around the world. This is called global warming. Any change in sea temperature is sure to affect sharks and other fishes. The increasing world population—and the pollution and development that go along with it—is definitely changing the habitats of

A BLUE SHARK GLIDES BENEATH A PATCH OF WEEDS IN THE OPEN OCEAN. BOTH THIS
ENVIRONMENT AND THE SHARKS THEMSELVES ARE TREASURES TO BE PRESERVED.

many shark species. For animals that have based their survival on living in a stable environment over millions of years, the threat from these changes is great. Of course, the environmental threats are to humans as well. If humans can solve these problems, they will help sharks by helping themselves.

Glossary

Ampullae of Lorenzini—Tiny pores located on the heads of sharks that detect electrical signals in the water

anal fin—A single fin located on the underside of certain fish, near the base of the tail

barbels—fleshy appendages, usually on a fish's lower jaw, used as "feelers" to sense prey

bubble curtain—A stream of bubbles that will sometimes deter fish. Used by whales to corral fish into a tight school, and unsuccessfully by humans as a deterrent to sharks.

buoyancy—the ability to float

cartilage— a tough but flexible material that forms the nose and ears in humans and the skeleton in sharks

caudal fin—the tail fin of a fish, usually used to power forward motion

chimaera—(pronounced kī-'mir-a) Also called the rattail, a relative of the shark—named after the mythological Greek monster that had the head of a lion, the body of a goat, and the tail of a dragon.

claspers—pair of sexual organs in male sharks

dermal denticles—tooth-like scales that cover the skin of sharks

dorsal fin—the fin along the back of a fish

gestation period—The length of time animals take to develop from conception to birth.

lateral line—A line of pores along the sides of fish that contain cells filled with hairs that are able to sense vibrations.

mermaid's purse—common name for the tough membrane that forms the egg case of some sharks, skates, and rays

nictitating membrane—a transparent membrane that covers the eyes of some sharks as protection when struggling with prey.

operculum—The single plate-like covering of bony fish that opens with the flow of water over the gills. In contrast, sharks have individual gill slits to allow the water to escape the gill chamber.

oviparous—The term for reproduction whereby the female lays eggs that will develop outside her body.

ovoviviparous—The term for reproduction whereby the female retains the egg inside her body.

pectoral fin—paired fins that are located on the sides of a fish's body, behind the gills

swim bladder—gas-filled organ in bony fish that helps them maintain buoyancy

viviparous—The term for reproduction whereby the female gives nourishment to the developing embryo through direct attachment to her body. This is similar to mammals with an umbilical cord

wobbegong—a species of highly camouflaged shark from Australia.

Species Checklist

The list below identifies the eight orders of sharks followed by some of the species discussed in this book. Scientific and common names are provided. The scientific name for a species includes the genus, which is capitalized, and the species, which is in lowercase. Both names are written in italics.

Hexanchiformes—the six- and seven-gill sharks sometimes called cow sharks and frilled sharks; two families, about five species

Chlamydoselachus anguineus	frilled shark
Hexanchus griseus	bluntnose six-gill shark

Squaliformes—the dogfish sharks; four families, about eighty-two species

Squalus acanthias	spiny dogfish
Squaliolus laticaudus	spined pygmy shark

Pristiophoriformes—the sawsharks; a single family, about five species

Pristiophorus nudipinnis	shortnose sawshark

Squatiniformes—the angel sharks; a single family, about thirteen species

Squatina squatina	angel shark

Heterodontiformes—the horned, or bullhead, sharks; one family, eight species.

Heterodontus portusjacksoni	Port Jackson shark
Heterodontus francisci	horned shark

Orectolobiformes—the carpet sharks; seven families about thirty-three species

Orectolobus ornatusornate	wobbegong
Ginglymostoma cirratum	nurse shark
Rhincodon typus	whale shark

Lamniformes—the Mackerel sharks; seven families, about sixteen species

Carcharias taurus	sand tiger or gray nurse shark
Cetorhinus maximus	basking shark
Mitsukurina owstoni	goblin shark
Megachasma pelagios	megamouth shark
Alopias vulpinus	thresher shark
Carcharodon carcharias	great white shark

Carcharhiniformes—the ground sharks, includes cat sharks and requiem sharks; seven families, approximately 197 species

Triakis semifaciata	leopard shark
Sphyrna mokarran	great hammerhead
Galeocerdo cuvier	tiger shark
Carcharhinus leucas	bull shark

Further Research

The books listed here are some of the many references available about sharks and shark attacks. A selection of videos and web sites is also included.

Books for Young People

Burnham, Brad. *The Sand Tiger Shark*. New York: The Rosen Publishing Group, 2001.

Bunting, Eve. *Sea World Book of Sharks*. San Diego: Harcourt Brace Jovanovich, Inc., 1979.

Cole, Joanna. *Hungry, Hungry Sharks*. New York: Random House, 1986.

Dozier, Thomas A. *Dangerous Sea Creatures*. New York: Time Life Books, 1976.

MacQuitty, Miranda. *Shark*. New York: Eyewitness Books, 1992

Oakley, M. *Shark*. New York:Ladybird Books, 1996.

Resnick, Jane P. *Sharks*. Chicago: Kidsbooks Inc., 1999.

Wexo, John Bonnett. *Sharks*. San Diego: Zoobooks, Wildlife Education Ltd., 1983.

Videos

The Hunt for the Great White Shark. National Geographic, 1994.

Shark Encounters. National Geographic, 1991.

The Sharks. National Geographic, 1982.

Web Sites

http://www.nationalgeographic.com/fieldtales/greatwhite/
Shows a great white shark attack, in which the shark lunges completely out of the water.

http://shark.co.za/
>Natal Shark Board of South Africa's infamous area noted for shark attacks. Gives history of efforts to study and conserve sharks, while preventing attacks on humans.

http://www.seaworld.org/Sharks/pageone.html
>Sea World's informative site for information about shark species.

http://www.pbs.org/oceanrealm/seadwellers/sharkdwellers/greatwhite1.html
>Public Broadcasting Station site with information on their features about the great white and other shark species.

http://www.rodneyfox.com.au/
>Site of Rodney Fox, the Australian diver who survived a massive attack by a great white shark.

http://www.flmnh.ufl.edu/fish/sharks/sharks.htm
>Site of the Florida Museum of Natural History where the International Shark Attack File (ISAF), a compilation of all known shark attacks, is administered in association with the American Elasmobranch Society. Gives other links for shark researchers.

Bibliography

Allen, Thomas B., *Shadows in the Sea*. New York: Lyons & Burford, 1996.

Allen, Thomas B. *Shark Almanac*. New York: Lyons Press, 1999.

Baldridge, David. H. *Shark Attack*. New York: Berkley Publishing, 1974.

Castro, Jose I. *The Sharks of North American Waters*. College Station, TX: Texas A&M University Press, 1983.

Cole, Joanna. *Hungry, Hungry Sharks*. New York: Random House, 1986.

Dozier, Thomas A. *Dangerous Sea Creatures*. New York: Time Life Books, 1976.

Ellis, Richard. *The Book of Sharks*. New York: Grosset and Dunlap, 1975.

Greenberg, Jerry & Idaz. *Fish Men Fear . . . Sharks!* Miami: Seahawk Press, 1969.

Gruber, Samuel H. *Discovering Sharks*. Highlands, NJ: American Littoral Society, 1990.

Helm, Thomas. *Shark! Unpredictable Killer of the Sea*. New York: Collier Books, 1961.

Johnson, R.H. *Sharks of Tropical and Temperate Seas*. Houston, TX: Pisces Books, 1995.

Kimley, A.P. and David G. Ainley. *Great White Shark*. San Diego: Academic Press, 1996

Lineweaver, Thomas H. III and Richard H. Bachus. *The Natural History of Sharks*. New York: Lyons & Burford, 1970.

MacQuitty, Miranda. *Shark*. New York: Alfred A Knopf, 1992.

McDiarmid, Mac. *Shark Attack*. New York: Smithmark Publishers,1996.

Stevens, John D. ed. *Sharks*. New York: Facts on File, 1987.

Index

Page numbers for illustrations are in **boldface**.

Ampullae of Lorenzini, 50, **51**, 72, 78, 96
angel sharks, **14**, 25–26, **28**, 39
attacks on humans
  by bull sharks, 80
  fatalities from, 84–87, 98
  by great whites, 75–77, 86, 94
  by hammerheads, 78
  locations of, 81, 84–85, 96–98
  numbers of, 10, 36
  by oceanic whitetips, 81
  protection from, 49–51, **59**, **83**, 90–98, **91**, **93**, **95**
  reasons for, 59, 80, 84–86
  reports of, 82–84, 96
  by tiger sharks, 79
  types of, 84–86

basking sharks, 12, **12**, 39, 44, 68–70, **69**
behavior, 45, 54–60, **58**, **61**, 68–79, 98
bioluminescent sharks, 70–73
blue sharks, 27, 39, **51**, 60, 65, **100**
body shapes, 26–31, **28–29**, 44, **48**
body temperatures, 41–42
bony fishes, 16–20, 34, 38, 44–46, 60, 87

breathing, 42–43
bull sharks, 13, 27, 36, 80, **81**
buoyancy, 38–41

Carcharodon megalodon, **21**, 37, **37**
carpet sharks, 26–27, **28**, 62, 68
cartilage, 18–22, 34, 42, 45
cat sharks, **12**, 27, 39, 62
chimaeras, 22–23, **22**
Cladoselache, 18, 20–21, 45
classification of sharks, **6–7**, 16, 20–22, 25–27, 31
cookie-cutter sharks, 35, 72–73, **73**

denticles, 20, 35
dogfish sharks, 30–31, **48**, **62–63**, 63, 74–75, **74**

early sharks, 18–20, 34, 37–38, 44–45, 61
eating of sharks, 87–89, **88**
electroreception, 50, **51**, 77, 95–96
evolution, 15–18, **19**, 25, 34–35, 44–46, 98
eyes, **19**, **24**, 26–27, 31, **31**

feeding frenzy, 58, **58**

feeding strategies, 45, 58, 68, 72–78
fins
  of angel sharks, 25
  attack behavior and, 59
  of bull sharks, 80
  of chimaeras, 22–23
  of dogfish sharks, 31, 75
  as food, 88–89, **88**
  of horned sharks and, 26
  of mackerel sharks, 26
  motion and, 39, **40**, 77
  of oceanic whitetips, **40**, 81
  of pygmy sharks, 74
  of rays, 23, **24**
  shark classification and, **19**, 25
  of whale sharks and, 27
fossils, 18–21, **21**, 34, 37–38, 45
frilled sharks, 26, 44, 65

gill rakers, 66, 70–71
gills, **19**, 23–26, **24**, 42–44, **42–43**, 89
goblin sharks, 72
great white sharks
  attacks by, 75–77, 86, 94
  camouflage of, 76–77, **76**
  Carcharodon megalodon and, 37
  feeding strategy of, 77, **85**, 88

hunting of, 89
jaws of, **17**
protection of, 89–90
range of, **14**, 75
reproduction of, 65
size of, 75–76
speed of, 76
teeth of, **17**, 36
ground sharks, 27, **29**, 31, **31**

habitats, 10–15, **12–14**, 26–27,
    37–39, 62, 68–80
hammerhead sharks, **11**, 27,
    36, 65, 77–79, **78**
hearing, 46–49
horned sharks, 26, **29**, 62
humans and sharks, 27, 66–68,
    80, 90, 98. *See also*
    attacks on humans
hunting of sharks, 41, 44, 74,
    87–89, 98–99

International Shark Attack File
    (ISAF), 82–86, 96

jaws, **17**, 18–20, 44, 71

lateral line, 48, 77
livers, 38–39, **42**

mackerel sharks, 26, **29**, 39–44
mako sharks, 26, **29**, **36**,
    39–41, 88
mating habits, 60, **61**
megamouth sharks, 37, 70–72,
    71
mermaid's purse, 62–63, **62**
Moses sole, 51, 91, **91**
mouths
    of basking sharks, **12**
    breathing and, 42–43
    of Carcharodon megalodon,
        37
    of carpet sharks, 26–27

of cookie-cutter sharks, 73,
    73
of early fish, 20
of frilled sharks, 44
of horned sharks, 26
jaws and, 20
location of, **19**, 26, **42**, 43,
    68
of megamouths, 70
of nurse shark, 84
of rays, **24**
of sand tiger sharks, **35**
shark classification and, **19**,
    25
smell and, 49
stomachs and, 53
taste and, 51
of whale sharks, 27, 66–68
movement, 23, 39, **40**, 44, **45**,
    77
muscles, 41–42, **41**

nictitating eyelid, **19**, 31, **31**
nurse sharks, **15**, 39, 43–45,
    45, 65, 84

oceanic whitetip sharks, 27, 40,
    55, 81

pilot fish, **55**
population numbers, 10,
    69–70, 74–75, 81, 89, 98
prey
    of basking sharks, 12, 44,
        68, 70
    of bull sharks, 80
    of Carcharodon megalodon,
        37
    of carpet sharks, 27
    catching of, 44–45
    of Cladoselache, 21
    of cookie-cutter sharks, 36,
        72
    feeding frenzy and, 58–60, **58**
    of hammerheads, 77

humans as, 36, 79–80,
    86–87
locating of, 49–50, 72,
    77–78, 97
of megamouths, 70
sharks as, 20, 60
teeth and, 35–36
of tiger sharks, **9**, 51, 53, 79
of whale sharks, 12, 66
protection of sharks, 87–90,
    98–99, 101
pygmy sharks, 12, 73–74

rattails, 22–23, **22**
rays, 18, 23–26, **24**
reef sharks, **13**, 27, **47**, 58, **61**
relatives of sharks, 18, 22–25,
    22, **24**
reproduction, 60–65, **62–63**,
    65, 68–70, 75, 79–80
requiem sharks, 27, 79–80

sand tiger sharks, **33**, **35**, 39,
    64, **65**
sawfish, 23, **24**, **25**, 26
saw sharks, 26, **28**
sea serpents, 71
sense of smell, 49–50
sense of taste, 51, 53
shark studies, 56–57, **57**, 70,
    77–79, 84, 89
six- or seven gill sharks, 26, 44
sizes, 12, **12**, 18, 26, 37, 64–81
skates, 23, **24**, 26
skeletons, 18, 20, 22, 34
skins, 35, 60, 86, 99
spines, 25–27, 30, 74–75
stomachs, **52**, 53
survival ability, 15, **17**, 32–34,
    33, 101
swimming speeds, 21, 25–26,
    39, 41, 44–45, 68–77

tails, 18, 23–26, 39, 44–45, **45**,
    77

teeth
  of blue sharks, 60
  of bull sharks, 36
  of carpet sharks, 27
  of chimaeras, 22
  of cookie-cutter sharks,
    72–73, **73**
  evolution of, 35
  fossils of, 18–21, **21**, 36–38
  of great whites, **17**, 36
  of hammerheads, 36
  of makos, **36**
  of nurse sharks, 84
  prey and, 35–36
  replacement of, 36, **38**
  of sand tiger sharks, **35**

of saw sharks, 26
of tiger sharks, 36, **38**, 79
use of, 35–36, **35–36**
tiger sharks
  attacks on humans, 79
  as ground sharks, 27
  habitat of, 79
  prey of, **9**, 51, 53, 79
  reproduction of, 65, 79–80
  as requiem sharks, 27
  stomachs of, **52**
  teeth of, 36, **38**, 79

whales, 36–37, 44, 66, 72–73
whale sharks
  breathing of, **43**, 66

as carpet sharks, 27, **28**, 68
feeding strategy of, 68
fins of, 27
habitat of, 68
humans and, 66–68
mouths of, 27, 66–68
nature of, 44
prey of, 12, 66
range of, **14**
reproduction of, 65, 68
size of, 12, 66, **67**
tails of, 44
wobbegongs, 27, 68

young sharks, **11**, **63**, 70,
  79–80

About the Author

PAUL L. SIESWERDA is currently curator of the New York Aquarium in Coney Island, New York. Previously, he was curator of Fishes and Mammals with the New England Aquarium in Boston, Massachusetts. Mr. Sieswerda has published numerous scientific papers and popular articles on marine subjects and has firsthand experience feeding sharks—with only a few scars to show for the effort.